DATE DUE

MR 2 0 '13		
DE - 9 '13		

WILEY

Wiley Publishing, Inc.

111 River Street
Hoboken, NJ 07030-5774

www.wiley.com

Copyright © 2011 by Wiley Publishing, Inc., Indianapolis, Indiana

Published by Wiley Publishing, Inc., Indianapolis, Indiana

Published simultaneously in Canada

WILEY

About the Author

Andy Harris once owned a TRS-80 Model I. It's still in the garage. He remembers fondly typing BASIC code into that machine and wondering how it really worked. He eventually taught himself enough programming to work as a consultant while pursuing a career in special education. He now teaches for Indiana University — Purdue University / Indianapolis as a Senior Lecturer in Computer Science. He teaches Web programming, game development, and Freshman Computer Science classes.

Dedication

I dedicate this book to Jesus Christ, my personal savior, and to Heather, the joy in my life. I also dedicate this project to Benjamin, Jacob, Matthew, and Elizabeth. I love each of you.

Author's Acknowledgments

People often think of writing as a solo sport, but I know better. Thanks to Heather, for being amazing (again and again). Thank you Katie Feltman, for another interesting project, and for being a consistent friend. Thanks to Blair Pottenger for all your support on this book. You wrestled this monster into decent shape. Thanks very much to Heidi Unger for your editing help. It took more than a minute to win this one. Thank you Ronald Norman for the technical edit. You found a number of goofy errors that would have confused students. Thank you so much for your vigilance.

Thanks also to the many people at Wiley who the author never gets to meet. I appreciate your contributions. Thank you also to the open-source community which creates so many excellent tools. A big thanks to the IUPUI family for supporting me through this and so many other projects, especially Michele and Lingma.

Finally, thank you to my extended family — the Friday morning guys, and the Sunday evening families. I'm lucky to have a job where I get to publicly thank you for all you add to my life.

Publisher's Acknowledgments

We're proud of this book; please send us your comments at http://dummies.custhelp.com. For other comments, please contact our Customer Care Department within the U.S. at 877-762-2974, outside the U.S. at 317-572-3993, or fax 317-572-4002.

Some of the people who helped bring this book to market include the following:

Acquisitions, Editorial, and Media Development

Project Editor: Blair J. Pottenger

Acquisitions Editor: Katie Feltman

Copy Editor: Heidi Unger

Technical Editor: Ronald Norman

Editorial Manager: Kevin Kirschner

Media Development Project Manager: Laura Moss-Hollister

Media Development Assistant Project Manager: Jenny Swisher

Media Development Associate Producers: Josh Frank, Marilyn Hummel, Douglas Kuhn, and Shawn Patrick

Editorial Assistant: Amanda Graham

Sr. Editorial Assistant: Cherie Case

Composition Services

Project Coordinator: Katie Crocker

Layout and Graphics: Erin Zeltner

Proofreaders: John Greenough, Sossity R. Smith

Indexer: Potomac Indexing LLC

Publishing and Editorial for Technology Dummies

Richard Swadley, Vice President and Executive Group Publisher

Andy Cummings, Vice President and Publisher

Mary Bednarek, Executive Acquisitions Director

Mary C. Corder, Editorial Director

Publishing for Consumer Dummies

Diane Graves Steele, Vice President and Publisher

Composition Services

Debbie Stailey, Director of Composition Services

A Note About the Term HTML5

As this book was nearing completion, the World Wide Web Consortium (W3C) announced that the change of the upcoming version of HTML would not be HTML5, but simply HTML. They reasoned that a collaborative project like an HTML standard is an evolution rather than a strict milestone. When HTML5 is reasonably universal, there will be no need to call it HTML5, but simple HTML will do.

For the purposes of this book, it is important to distinguish between the current state of the art and the evolving standard that is the focus of this work. For that reason, I refer to the emerging standards as HTML5 to distinguish them from the older approaches to Web development, and keep the term HTML5 in the title.

Companion Resources On the Web

Be sure to check out my Web site for working examples of every code fragment in the book: www.aharrisbooks.net/h5qr.

Also check out this book's companion Web site at www.dummies.com/go/html5fdqr to access "Bonus Part 1: Using JavaScript" for a review (or preview) of computer programming in JavaScript. Programming is a complex business, and learning how to program in JavaScript deserves its own book; see my *JavaScript and AJAX For Dummies* (Wiley) or *HTML, XHTML, and CSS All-In-One For Dummies, 2nd edition* (Wiley) books for a more complete treatment.

Table of Contents

Part 1

Moving on to HTML5

HTML5 is the newest incarnation of the HTML family of languages. HTML, which stands for HyperText Markup Language, is one of the main reasons the Web is as powerful and useful as it is. HTML is a reasonably simple system of plain-text codes that provide the structure of all Web pages on the Internet.

In this part, you take a quick look at how HTML5 fits in the history of the Web, and put together a few tools you'll need to get started.

Be sure to check out my Web site for working examples of every code fragment in the book: www.aharrisbooks.net/h5qr.

In this part . . .

- ✔ **Looking at the History of HTML**
- ✔ **Understanding What HTML5 Is**
- ✔ **Running Tests for Browser Features**
- ✔ **Deciding on a Suitable Browser**
- ✔ **Utilizing Chrome Frame to Add Support to IE**

A Quick History of HTML

HTML is a key part of the Internet. It has a short but extremely vibrant history. In order to understand what HTML5 is about, it's useful to look at where it came from. The Internet (and the Web in particular) has been changing at a dizzying pace. HTML has been trying to keep up.

When HTML was first devised, it comprised a handful of tags, and HTML did little more than determine how a page was laid out. As the Web matured, many features were added. Today's Internet is still about documents, but it's also about applications. Today's Web sites are dynamic interactive applications.

The kinds of devices used on the Internet are changing, too. In the early days, only desktop computers used the Web. Now cellphones and mobile devices are among the most important players on the Web. They require a different way of thinking than the standard desk-based behemoths of a few years ago.

It's time for a fresh new set of standards that will help support the way people are using the Internet today. HTML5 is that set of standards.

A bit of ancient history

In the distant mists of time (1989) Tim Berners-Lee created a new system of connecting electronic documents. He devised a simple language that allowed document authors to link various documents together with limited formatting options. This language was called HTML.

At that point, the Internet existed, but it was mainly accessed by basic command-line programs, and was not easy to use. HTML (and some other underlying technologies) was designed from the beginning to be easy to work with, and to create documents that were easy for users to manage. The design of HTML was deliberately kept simple, so as many people as possible could participate in the process of building documents in this new format.

Of course, the Web took off in a very major way, and soon Web pages became ubiquitous. It became clear that the simple features in basic HTML were not enough to satisfy the interests of the many people who were now building Web pages.

And the first browser war begins . . .

As various organizations started building *Web browsers* (the tools that read HTML and display it to the user), they began competing by adding new HTML features. By 1993, the Mosaic browser included the ability to add images (which were not part of the original specification). Many browsers were being created by small teams all around the world, and each had its own set of new features.

By 1994, one platform emerged as the dominant browser. Netscape Navigator was a profoundly successful browser. At the same time, there were working groups forming to address the lack of standards in the Web browser world. The most important of these groups was called the World Wide Web Consortium (W3C) headed by Tim Berners-Lee (the same guy who started all this mess). However, Netscape had such a dominant position that Netscape representatives often skipped the standards meetings and created whatever features they wanted.

Microsoft did not come into the browser world until 1995. Internet Explorer (IE) was designed to compete directly with Netscape's browser. For a time (sometimes called the first browser wars), Netscape and Microsoft were in an arms race, each trying to produce exclusive features that would steer developers toward their own vision of the Web.

While there was a standards body in place, the reality was both Netscape and Microsoft added whatever features they wanted and basically ignored the W3C. There was some small progress made on Web standards. HTML 2 was adopted as a standard in 1994/1995 (although none of the manufacturers stuck with it completely). HTML 3.2 was released in 1997, followed by HTML 4 in Spring of 1998.

By about the same time HTML 4 was gaining traction, it became clear that Microsoft was dominating the browser space. By 2002, Internet Explorer was used by approximately 95 percent of Internet users. With that kind of clout, the future of HTML was almost entirely in Microsoft's hands, and efforts of standards bodies were largely irrelevant. By any measure, Microsoft won the first browser war. Internet Explorer 6 (which used mainly HTML 4) was the only browser that really mattered, and there was very little innovation for several years.

A new challenger arises from the ashes

However, there were some new browsers that challenged Microsoft's dominance. The Firefox browser (first released in 2004) in particular was especially important, as it introduced a number of innovative features and followed most of the standards of the W3C working group. Firefox (and to a lesser extent other browsers like Apple's Safari, Opera, and eventually Google Chrome) shook up the Web. These other browsers tended to be more committed to following standards than IE was, and they prompted new versions of IE following a long era of stagnation. Even Microsoft began to at least pay lip service to the notion of standards, promising more standards compliance in each of the new versions of IE introduced. Some consider this the opening of the second browser war, with various developers competing for share of the browser market.

However, there is a difference this time around. The Web is no longer a novelty, but now a key part of business and society. A Web-based document is now held to the same visual standards as printed documents, and HTML 4 is simply not capable of easily meeting this standard. In fact, the entire notion of the Web as a series of documents is being challenged. Web *pages* are being replaced by Web *applications*. Much of what people now do on the Internet isn't about reading documents any more. Today, developers are using the Web itself as a programming interface.

HTML 4 was getting old

Changes in the Web required a change in the thinking about document standards. HTML 4 was clearly not up to the task of supporting modern Web development. The various proprietary tags added through the years added some visual flexibility, but not nearly enough. There was not a satisfying solution for page layout or font management. There was a set of features for entering form data, but these tools were limited and ugly. Most browsers featured a form of the JavaScript programming language, but the implementations varied wildly, and making a real application using Web technologies was a chancy proposition.

The W3C introduced XHTML in 2002 to address some of these concerns. XHTML was proposed as a version of HTML adhering to the stricter standards of the XML markup language. XHTML is much less forgiving than HTML, so if a page meets the stringent requirements of the standard, it is (presumably) well-behaved and predictable. Unfortunately, the idealism of the XHTML movement was never realized. Creating valid XHTML documents proved difficult enough that very few developers tried. Browsers rendered inaccurate XHTML code decently (if not perfectly). In fact, most browsers didn't really render XHTML at all, but quietly converted it to a form of HTML. There was little incentive for developers to adhere to XHTML standards (unless they were taking my class).

In order to get the functionality that was missing from HTML, many developers turned to plug-in technology like Java Applets and embedded Flash. Java never caught on as a client-side environment (although it remains extremely important in other applications) but Flash was very popular for a time. Unfortunately, Flash introduces problems of its own. The content of a Flash applet can only be modified by a Flash editor, and it cannot be read (at least easily) by search engines. Many of the new features of HTML5 (particularly the font support and the canvas tag) can be seen as a direct response to Flash.

The W3C moved to create a new form of XHTML called XHTML 2.0, but in the mean time, a second group called WHATWG (Web Hypertext Application Technology Working Group) began working on their own competing standard, which came to be known as HTML5. The main reason for these competing standards was a sense that XHTML was too rigid, and was still focused on HTML as a document language. Part of the motivation for HTML5 was to create a framework for building Web applications that would really be used by developers. Eventually, W3C dropped support for XHTML 2 and is now supporting the WHATG proposal, so HTML5 appears to be the next standard.

Getting to Know the Real HTML5

The WHATWG group seems to have learned a few lessons from history. The design of HTML5 indicates these priorities:

✔ **The core language should be simple.** HTML5 is quite a bit cleaner than XHTML. The document type in particular is a breath of fresh air compared to the nonsense you have to write to start an XHTML page. Every tag is about describing some feature of the page. Most of the tags are plain English with few abbreviations.

✔ **Markup is based on semantics.** One of the original ideas in HTML was markup based on *meaning* rather than *details*. For example, a headline is simply marked as <h1> rather than specifying a particular font size or typeface. HTML5 returns to this tradition, adding a number of new tags to describe common parts of a page.

✔ **CSS is used for style details.** Like XHTML, HTML5 relies heavily on another language, called CSS (Cascading Style Sheets), to handle the details of how a particular element looks. In essence, HTML describes *what* a page element is, and CSS describes *how* that element looks. HTML5 does not contain tags like <font> or <center> because these characteristics are handled in a more flexible way by CSS.

✔ **Pages are often applications.** *Forms* (the elements that allow users to enter data in a Web site) have been a part of HTML since the beginning, but they have not seen much improvement over the years. HTML5 adds a number of very exciting new form elements that make HTML a much better tool for interacting with users.

✔ **JavaScript is central.** Most Web browsers have had a form of the JavaScript (JS) programming language built in for years. However, it was difficult to take JavaScript very seriously because it had a number of limitations. Some limitations were because of legitimate security concerns, and others were simply poor or incompatible implementation. With the advent of new powerful JavaScript engines and a new paradigm called AJAX (Asynchronous JavaScript and XML), JavaScript has re-emerged as a powerful and important programming environment. Many of the most interesting features of HTML5 (like the canvas tag) are mainly improvements in the JavaScript language. (The canvas tag is an HTML tag, but it doesn't do anything interesting without JavaScript.)

HTML5 Is More than HTML!

It's a little unfortunate that this technology has been called HTML5, because the HTML language is actually only one part of a much bigger picture. In truth, the thing we call HTML5 is the integration of several different technologies (HTML, CSS, and JavaScript, and server-based technologies), which each have their own role as follows:

HTML

Of course, there have been changes to the HTML language itself. A few tags have been added to the HTML 4 standard, and a number have been taken away. However, HTML5 remains backwards-compatible with HTML 4, so there's no absolute requirement to write your code in the HTML5 standard. Adapting from HTML 4 to HTML5 is probably the easiest part of moving to the complete HTML mindset.

Here are the main HTML features:

- **Semantic markup:** HTML5 now includes new tags that describe parts of a document. Now there are dedicated tags for navigation elements, articles, sections, headers, and footers.

- **New form elements:** HTML5 forms have some major updates. There are several new versions of the `<input>` element, allowing users to pick colors, numbers, e-mail addresses, and dates with easy-to-use elements.

- **Media elements:** At long last, HTML5 has native support for audio and video with tags similar to the `<img>` tag.

- **canvas tag:** The `canvas` tag allows the programmer to build graphics interactively. This capability will allow for very intriguing capabilities like custom gaming and interface elements.

CSS

Probably the biggest adjustment for those used to HTML 4 isn't really the HTML itself, but the changing relationship between HTML and CSS. In HTML5 (like in XHTML), the markup language only describes what various elements mean. CSS is used to describe how things look. If you're really going to switch to HTML5, you can no longer use tags like `<font>` and `<center>`, which are about describing details. CSS could be considered an optional add-on to HTML 4, but it's central to the HTML5 way of thinking. If you haven't yet learned CSS, it's definitely time. CSS is a different way of thinking, but it's incredibly powerful and flexible. Along with the HTML5 standard comes a new standard for CSS, called CSS3. It's nearly impossible to talk about HTML5 without also including CSS3 because they're so closely related. Here are the main new features:

- **Embedded font support:** With this long-awaited tool, you can include a font with a Web page, and it will render even if the user doesn't have the font installed on her operating system.

- **New selectors:** Selectors are used to describe a chunk of code to be modified. CSS3 now supports new selectors that let you choose every other element, as well as specific sub-elements (different types of input tags, for example).

- **Columns:** HTML has never had decent support for columns, and all kinds of hacks have been used to overcome this shortcoming. Finally, CSS includes the ability to break an element into any number of columns easily.

  ✔ **Visual enhancements:** CSS has a number of interesting new capabilities: transparency, shadows, rounded corners, animations, gradients, and transformations. These provide a profound new level of control over the appearance of a page.

JavaScript

If HTML describes what parts of the document are, and CSS describe how these parts look, JavaScript is used to define how elements act. JavaScript is a full-blown programming language, and it deserves its own book (which, of course it has; look to my book *JavaScript and AJAX For Dummies* [Wiley] for one example). It is not possible to describe JavaScript completely in this reference guide, but JavaScript is a very critical part of the HTML5 point of view. A few of HTML5's most interesting features (the canvas tag, geolocation, and local data storage, for example) are accessible only through JavaScript. I describe these features in this book. *See* Bonus Part 1 for an overview of JavaScript if you need a review or an introduction.

  ✔ **Vector graphics support:** Vector-based graphics provide an interesting alternative to traditional graphics because they can be created on the fly through code. HTML5 actually has two ways to do this: through SVG (Scalable Vector Graphics) and the canvas tag.

  ✔ **New selectors:** Most JavaScript programming begins by grabbing an element by ID. HTML5 now allows you to select elements by tag name, or by the same mechanisms you use to select elements in CSS.

  ✔ **Local storage mechanisms:** Previous versions of HTML allowed very limited storage of information on the client. HTML5 now allows the developer to store data on the client. There is even a built-in database manager that accepts SQL commands.

  ✔ **Geolocation:** This interesting feature uses a variety of mechanisms to determine where the user is located.

Server technologies

Modern Web development is about communication. All of the technologies that make up HTML5 reside in the Web browser, which is an important part of the Web. However, an equally important part of Web development is a raft of technologies that live on the Web server. Many of the most interesting things happening today use technologies like PHP or ASP to run programs that create Web pages. Many interesting applications also use database programs like Oracle or MySQL to manage large amounts of data. The advent of AJAX has made integration between those technologies and the browser much easier. Interesting as these tools are, I do not focus on them in this reference book. If you're interested in them, please see my book *HTML, XHTML, CSS All-in-One For Dummies* (Wiley) for a thorough treatment of these and other topics.

Looking At Browser Features

As you can see in the history of HTML, calling something a standard doesn't make it so. Officially, HTML5 hasn't been accepted yet, and there isn't a single popular browser that implements all of its features. If that's the case, you might wonder if it's worth it to study this technology yet. I think so, for these reasons:

- ✔ **Most of the ideas are accepted.** While HTML5 itself has not yet been ratified as a formal standard, most of the critical ideas are available today. Today's Web browsers will work fine with HTML5 even if they don't know how to do all the cool things with it.

- ✔ **There is little doubt that HTML5 is the new standard.** W3C has essentially conceded that XHTML 2.0 is not a viable solution, leaving HTML5 as the clear winner in the standards war. If there is to be any standard at all, HTML5 (and the related features in CSS and JS) is it.

- ✔ **Standards-compliance is now a desirable feature.** In the first browser war, manufacturers were competing to add new features without any regard to standards. Today, browsers are judged by their adherence to accepted Web standards. Even Microsoft has gotten into the mix, claiming that IE 9 supports a majority of the HTML5 features.

- ✔ **HTML5 promotes good coding habits.** The separation of content from layout is a critical part of modern Web development. If you're coming from XHTML, you're already comfortable with this situation. If you're more familiar with HTML 4, it's a new idea, but one that has been inevitable.

Officially, HTML5 is not expected to be completely accepted as a standard until 2022. This seems like an eternity in Web time. However, parts of the standard (such as the `canvas` tag) are universally available right now and are worth exploring immediately. Others (like most of the form elements and the semantic markup tags) provide suitable backups automatically if the browser doesn't support the advanced features. Others (like drag-and-drop) are simply not ready for use yet. A few (like the local data support mechanism) are hotly debated, and it is not clear which form of the technology will become part of the standard. As I discuss each of these topics throughout the book, I try to give you a sense of whether it is ready to be used yet, and which browsers support particular features.

Assessing your browser's capabilities

HTML5 has a lot of different technologies going on, and different browsers have adopted different parts of the standards. It can be very confusing to determine which features can be used. There are a couple of good solutions to this problem. A number of sites have charts that indicate which features are supported in which browser. I like the ones at `http://caniuse.com` and `http://en.wikipedia.org/wiki/Comparison_of_layout_engines_%28HTML5%29`. These tools can help you see what is currently supported by the major browsers. It's especially handy for checking browsers you don't have on your own machine.

However, browser support for HTML5 features literally changes every day. New versions of major browsers are appearing all the time, and it's very hard to keep track of what's currently happening. For that reason, I've provided you with a program you can use to check your current browser to see which HTML5 features it supports. Figure 1-1 shows the detect.html program in action.

Figure 1-1

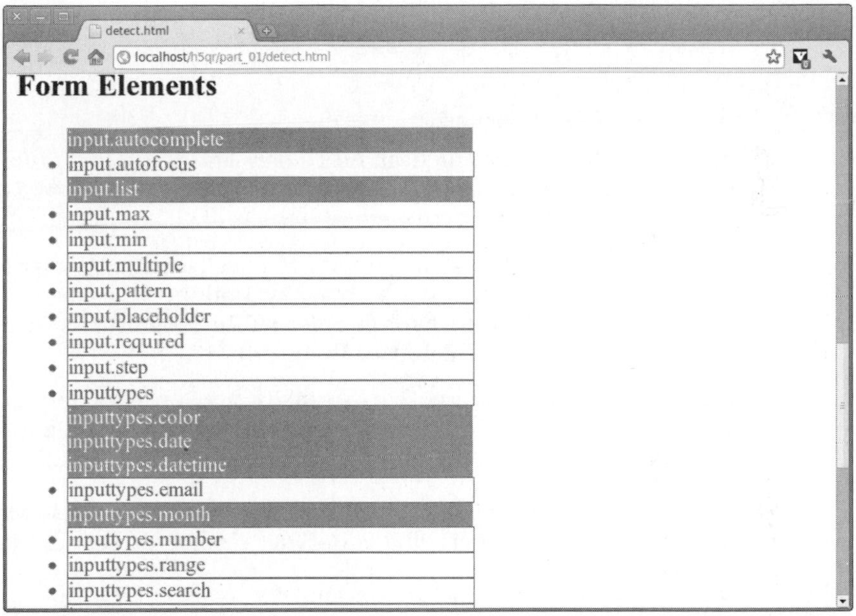

The detect.html page can be found at my Web site, www.aharrisbooks.net/ h5qr/detect.html. Use it with any browser to get real-time analysis of which HTML5 features are available in your browser.

The program uses a script called Modernizr, which automates checking for various browser features. You can get Modernizr for free from www.modernizr.com.

Checking for features in your code

You can also use the Modernizr script in your own code. Essentially, Modernizr creates a Boolean (true/false) value for each of the HTML features. You can check a variable to see if the current browser supports a particular feature. If it does, you can implement the feature. If not, you will generally implement some sort of fallback. Here's how it's done:

1. Download the Modernizr script. The Modernizr script can be downloaded free from www.modernizr.com. Install the script in the same directory as your Web page. (If you move your page to a server, you'll also need to make a copy of the script available.)

2. Include a reference to the script. Use the `<script>` tag to make a reference to the script in your header (before any other JavaScript code):

```
<script type = "text/javascript"
        src = "modernizr-1.6.min.js"></script>
```

3. Add a special class to the HTML tag. The Modernizr script needs to have a special tag available so it knows what to do. Add the "no-js" class to the HTML tag:

```
<html lang = "en"
      class = "no-js">
```

4. Write a new JavaScript function. Add a new JavaScript function to do the actual testing. Specific examples are shown in the code listing later in this section.

5. Use the appropriate Boolean property to check for a particular feature. Each of the HTML5 features supported by Modernizr has a corresponding variable. (You can look up the variables on the Modernizr site, or look at my detect.html script, which uses them all.)

6. Use the feature or an alternative. Normally, you'll use Modernizr to check for a feature. If that feature exists, you'll use it. If not, you'll implement some other alternative.

As an example, the following page uses the Modernizr script to test whether the current browser supports the HTML5 `video` tag. If so, it also checks for support of the two main video codecs.

```
<!DOCTYPE HTML>
<html lang = "en"
      class = "no-js">
<head>
  <title>checkVideo.html</title>
  <meta charset = "UTF-8" />
    <script type = "text/javascript"
            src = "modernizr-1.6.min.js"></script>
    <script type = "text/javascript">
      function init(){
        var output = document.getElementById("output");
        if (Modernizr.video){
          output.innerHTML =
          "Your browser supports video <br /> ";
          if (Modernizr.video.h264){
            output.innerHTML += "H.264 codec supported <br
/>";
```

```
        } // end if
        if (Modernizr.video.ogg){
          output.innerHTML +=
          "Ogg Theora video codec supported <br />";
        } // end if
      } else {
        output.innerHTML = "Your browser does not support
the HTML5 video tag";         } // end if
      } // end init
  </script>
</head>

<body onload = "init()">
  <h1>Check for HTML5 Video</h1>
  <div id = "output">
    checking video...
  </div>
</body>
</html>
```

Figure 1-2 shows the video-checking script in action.

Figure 1-2

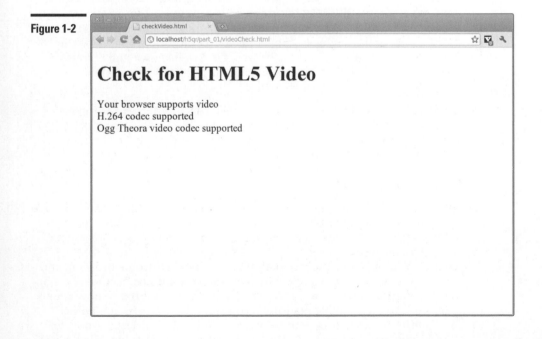

This example simply checks for the support for the video elements. A more sophisticated example would actually embed the appropriate tags or code in the page to display a video according to the browser's capabilities.

For more information on the video tag, please check Part 3.

Picking a Suitable Browser

If you're going to be writing HTML5 code, you'll probably want to view your pages in a browser that interprets HTML5 correctly. That's not as easy as it sounds. HTML5 isn't really one specification, but a number of different standards. The various browsers have differing versions of support. It's best to have a wide variety of browsers to see which one works best for you. There are several browsers currently available, which all have varying levels of HTML5 support.

While there are a large number of browsers available, most are based on a smaller set of tools called *rendering engines.* It's the rendering engine that really supports features or not. Here is a list of the primary engines, the browsers that use them, and how well they support HTML5:

- **Gecko (Firefox):** The Gecko engine is the main engine of Firefox, Mozilla, and a number of other related browsers. It has support for many, but not all features. Gecko 2.0 is expected to include most features of HTML5, but that version of the engine is not yet released (and will probably be the foundation of Firefox 4). Although Firefox is a well-known and respected browser in the Web development community, it does not (yet) have extremely good support for HTML5.

- **Trident (Internet Explorer):** The various forms of Internet Explorer all use the Trident engine. So far, this engine has the weakest support of HTML5 features among all the major browsers. IE9 promises to have much more complete support for HTML5, but even this version is projected to be missing some key features, including advanced form element support and geolocation.

- **WebKit:** The WebKit engine was originally created by Apple based on code from the open source KHTML project. Apple then released the code as open source, where it became the foundation of a number of browsers. The Safari browser on Macs, iPhones, and iPads all uses the WebKit engine. WebKit is also the foundation of the Google Chrome browser, and the browser on the Android mobile platform. WebKit has become the standard rendering engine for mobile platforms. If you want to see how your pages will look on mobile platforms, you should check with a WebKit-based browser like Chrome or Safari. WebKit has the widest support for HTML5 elements, although it still doesn't support everything. Most of the code in this book was tested in Google Chrome 6, which supports the cur-rent WebKit rendering engine.

✔ **Presto:** The Presto engine is the engine underlying the Opera family of browsers. Opera has long been considered a technically superior browser, but it has never gotten the market share it should. A number of gaming and portable browsers are based on Presto, including the Wii Internet Channel, the Nintendo DS Browser, and Opera Mobile, available on numerous cell-phones and portable devices.

Browser specifications are likely to change. It's likely that new features have been added by the time you read this book. You should always test your page in as many browsers as you can, so you won't be surprised. You might also check `http://en.wikipedia.org/wiki/Comparison_of_layout_engines_ (HTML5)`. This Wikipedia site tends to have the latest information on what fea-tures of HTML are supported by which browser.

Using Chrome Frame to Add Support to IE

It might be depressing to note that the browser with the largest market share has the least support for HTML5 standards. However, there is an answer. Google Chrome Frame is a special tool that embeds the Chrome rendering engine inside IE. To use it, put the following code in your page:

```
<!DOCTYPE html>
<html lang="en">
<head>
    <title>ChromeFrame.html</title>
    <meta charset="UTF-8">
  <script type="text/javascript"
          src="http://ajax.googleapis.com/ajax/libs/chrome-
frame/1/CFInstall.min.js"></script>
</head>

<body onload = "CFInstall.check()">
</body>

</html>
```

The rest of your code can be written assuming the user has Chrome (which has excellent support for HTML5). This is the best way to use HTML5 in IE until Microsoft decides to add meaningful support to HTML5.

Part 2

HTML Foundations

HTML5 is the latest of a series of HTML versions. To get the most out of HTML5, you need to know how it fits in with the other versions of HTML that came before it.

Most of this chapter is a review of standard HTML ideas. If you've never written any HTML by hand before, you'll want to look it over carefully. If you're already a code ace, you can probably just skim over it.

The content of this chapter forms a baseline. The code described here works in all modern browsers. As much of the HTML5 content is still browser-dependent, begin with a standard set of tags and elements that work on every browser. This chapter describes this lowest-common-denominator HTML syntax, which is expanded upon throughout the book.

This chapter is really an overview. If you're totally new to HTML, you might consider looking over one of my other books — *HTML, XHTML, and CSS All-in-One For Dummies,* 2nd edition (Wiley). It goes into great detail on HTML, CSS, and lots of other good stuff. That book is a standard reference for today's Web. The book you're holding now is really more about where the Web is going in the near future.

Be sure to check out my Web site for working examples of every code fragment in the book: www.aharrisbooks.net/h5qr.

In this part . . .

- ✔ Reviewing HTML
- ✔ Comparing HTML5 to XHTML and HTML 4
- ✔ Building the Basic Page
- ✔ Adding Images and Links
- ✔ Formatting Data with Lists and Tables
- ✔ Validating Your Code
- ✔ Building Forms

Exploring HTML and XHTML

HTML has been around for a while now, and it has been continuously changing. Ideas that were once cutting edge (like using frames) are now considered out of date. HTML began as a very simple language, which became more complex as it was used more. HTML5 tries to make HTML simple again. The following ideas have driven the development of HTML5.

✔ **Make the code as clean as possible.** Things will get complicated fast. HTML code should be clean and easy to read. It shouldn't have any unnecessary features, and it should be formatted in a way that is easy to follow.

✔ **Separate structure from design.** Try to keep your HTML code focused on the structure of the code (what it means) rather than the display (how it looks). This keeps the HTML code relatively clean and easy to work with.

✔ **Use HTML for structure.** Avoid tags like <font> and <center> in your HTML code, as they are difficult to change with JavaScript, clutter up your code, and are not allowed in some forms of HTML. Use HTML code to determine the meaning and structure of the page.

✔ **Use CSS for design.** You can keep the HTML a lot easier to work with if you leave the design work (colors, fonts, positions, and so on) to CSS. If you use CSS for design, your JavaScript will have a lot more ability to change how the page works because you can also modify CSS through JavaScript.

✔ **Avoid use of tables and frames for layout.** These techniques were the best tools Web designers had at one point, and so they were frequently used to provide visual structure to Web pages. However, modern CSS approaches provide for much cleaner code that's easier to work with even when things get more advanced.

✔ **Start with valid code.** A lot of times, a page will look perfectly fine, but there will be some mistake hidden away that will rear its ugly head at the worst possible time (usually when you're trying to show something to a client). It's best to start your projects with HTML that you know is valid. *See* "Validating Your Pages," later in this part, for more on ensuring the HTML foundation is in tip-top shape.

Appreciating HTML

HTML 4 was the dominant form of HTML for a long time. It was popular for some very good reasons:

✔ **Universal support:** By the time HTML 4 came out, there was really only one dominant browser — Internet Explorer 6 (IE6). Since the vast majority of users had some form of this browser, any code that would work for this browser was considered standard. In fact, the standards we call HTML 4 are really the parts of HTML 4 that were supported by IE6.

✔ **Reasonable control:** HTML 4 enhanced older versions of HTML with some nice features like font support, the ability to change colors, and some support for multimedia. Frames added a certain amount of layout support, although they brought their own problems.

✔ **Ease of use:** The HTML 4 standard itself was pretty easy to learn. It wasn't too much trouble until you tried to do advanced stuff like table-based layouts. Then the simplicity of the language began to hurt because it just couldn't do some things.

✔ **Forgiving:** HTML was designed to be very easygoing. If you did something wrong, the browser would simply guess what you were trying to say. Often, the guesses were correct.

Emergence of XHTML

HTML 4 was popular for a long time, but it wasn't perfect. As Web development moved from a hobby enterprise to become the foundation of serious applications, the weaknesses of HTML 4 became more apparent. While HTML 4 never died away, a new standard called XHTML (eXtensible HyperText Markup Language) emerged among elite Web developers. XHTML was intended as a more serious answer to HTML 4. While HTML 4 was easy to get along with, it was considered sloppy by professional programmers. XHTML (especially the strict version) was much more precise and predictable, making it popular among higher-end developers. Here are the key features of XHTML Strict:

✔ **More demanding syntax:** XHTML is case-sensitive, it requires all attributes to be encased in quotes, and it has very strict rules for how tags are nested. Every tag must have an explicit closing tag. (Even one-off tags like `<img>` require a special closing character.) This more precise syntax made XHTML a little more exacting to program than HTML 4, but the results were far more predictable.

✔ **Validation support:** The main advantage of all the strictness in XHTML was support for validation. The HTML 4 standard was so loosey-goosey that nobody could tell if a page was formatted incorrectly. With XHTML, it became possible to run a special validation program that could find structural errors in your code.

✔ **Separation of content and layout:** HTML was originally intended only to describe the content of a document. By the time HTML 4 came out, it added numerous tags for handling the visual aspects of a document. The `<font>` and `<center>` tags were prime examples of this. While these tags did their jobs, they did not provide enough control, and moved away from the central idea of HTML. XHTML strict removed all layout tags.

✔ **Rising importance of CSS:** Cascading Style Sheets (CSS) were available in HTML 4, but they were not always used properly because HTML provided some alternatives. When XHTML eliminated layout tags, CSS moved from an optional enhancement to a central part of Web development.

✔ **XML syntax:** Early promoters of XHTML emphasized that XHTML followed the syntax of the XML standard. While this is true, it never turned out to be quite as important as people thought it might. The XML syntax made it easier for automated programs to manipulate Web pages as data, but that's not a feature that most Web developers are terribly concerned about.

It's alive, and it's HTML5!

XHTML Strict was a really great idea, but it never really caught on. Professional developers (especially those who were integrating programming languages like JavaScript and PHP into their web projects) loved XHTML Strict. Top designers enjoyed the newfound freedom of CSS. However, XHTML was a little too unforgiving for most developers, and the vast majority of pages never bothered to validate to the new standards. When the time came to devise a new standard, the W3C finally decided to support HTML5 rather than XHTML 2.

HTML5 is not really a rejection of XHTML. It has some of the best features of both HTML 4 and XHTML:

✔ **Simple doctype:** The *doctype definition* (the boilerplate code that begins every Web page) for XHTML was really complicated. Even people who taught classes and wrote books about it (like, um, me) never memorized the doctype, but had to copy and paste it every time. HTML5 has a very simple and clean document definition, and it's once again possible to write a page with a text editor from memory.

✔ **Separation of content and style:** HTML5 does not include the style tags from HTML 4 (font, center, and so on), requiring developers to use CSS for all styling. Likewise, frames and table-based layout are discouraged in favor of CSS-style layout.

✔ **Validation support:** Validation turned out to be a very useful tool, so HTML5 can be validated just like XHTML. The W3C validator (http://validator. w3.org; *see* "Validating Your Pages" later in this part) supports HTML5 now, and other validation tools are coming online. Validation is an easy way to eliminate goofy coding mistakes, and can greatly simplify your coding once you start adding programming support to your documents.

✔ **Strict tradition:** The coding standards of HTML5 are more like XHTML than HTML 4. While it's still possible to use sloppy coding in HTML5, most developers use the XHTML strict standards to make the code easier to read and more predictable.

All the code in this book adheres to the stricter style standards of XHTML.

✔ **Tighter integration of CSS and programming languages:** Perhaps the most important feature of HTML5 is its humility. While HTML is still the central language of the Internet, HTML5 is really about distributing control to other languages. HTML5 is designed as a central glue that ties together many other technologies: CSS for visual layout, JavaScript for client-side programming, server-side languages like PHP for server control, and databases.

✔ **New capabilities:** Of course, HTML5 presents new capabilities, which are the primary focus of this book. Many of the new features are not technically HTML but advances in the various other related technologies (integrated databases, new JavaScript syntax, new CSS features, and so on).

Setting up a basic HTML page

The basic HTML5 page is quite easy to build. Just open up any text editor and add the following code:

```
<!DOCTYPE HTML>
<html lang = "en">
<head>
  <!-- basic.html -->
  <title>basic.html</title>
  <meta charset = "UTF-8" />
</head>

<body>
  <h1>Level One Headline</h1>

  <p>
    This is a paragraph.
    Note that the text is automatically wrapped.
  </p>

</body>
</html>
```

This page, shown in Figure 2-1, is not difficult to create:

 I tend to bump up the font sizes in these screenshots when I can — doing so makes the page a bit easier to read. Be sure to look at the actual page on the Web site (www.aharrisbooks.net) to see exactly how it works.

Figure 2-1

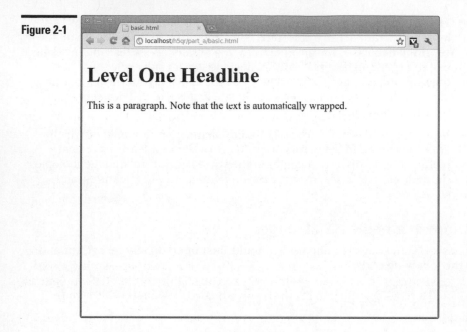

To build a basic HTML5 page, follow these steps:

1. Begin with the doctype. Modern versions of HTML (XHTML and HTML5) have a special attribute called the `doctype`, which indicates which form of HTML is being used. The doctype for XHTML was extremely confusing, and HTML 4 didn't have a doctype at all. Set the doctype to HTML5 with this tag: `<!DOCTYPE HTML>`. The doctype definition should be on the first line of your Web site. If you leave this out, you will still probably be able to use HTML5 features, but validators will have to guess about which form of HTML you're using. (Consult any science fiction movie to see what happens when computers make guesses about things.)

2. Add the `<html>` tag. This special tag indicates the beginning of a Web page. It's best to indicate which language the page is written in. Specify `lang = "en"` for English. Be sure to have a corresponding `</html>` tag at the bottom of the page. This indicates the end of the page you began with the `<html>` tag at the beginning of the page.

3. Create a `<head>` area. The head is something like the engine compartment of a car. People don't usually go there, but there's lots of important machinery. The head is empty in this simple example, but it will fill up with JavaScript and CSS goodness soon enough.

4. Specify the character set. While this isn't strictly necessary, it's considered good form to let the browser know what kind of characters to use when displaying your page. Pages written in English should generally use UTF-8, so indicate this with the following code: `<meta charset = "UTF-8" />`.

5. Indent your code. Browsers don't care if your code is indented, but it's a very good habit to get into. Generally, I indent every time I open a new element that isn't closed on the same line. Then it's easy for me to line up my beginning and ending tags to ensure the page is well formed and I didn't miss any ending tags.

6. Add a comment. Comments aren't strictly required, but they're very good form. HTML comments begin with `<!--` and end with `-->`. Typically the comments in this book will be a brief summary of the purpose of the page. Comments can last over several lines.

7. Put in a title with `<title></title>`. This tag allows you to specify a title for your page. The title typically appears in the Web browser's title bar, and will also often appear in search engine results for your page. In this book, I generally put the filename in the title, so you can easily match the programs on the book's companion Web site with those in the book code listings.

8. Include the bulk of the page in the `<body>` tags. If the `head` area is the engine compartment, the `body` is the passenger space. Most of the text that's visible on the Web site is part of the body. The `</body>` tag is usually right before the `</html>` tag, as you'll typically finish off the body and then close off the HTML.

9. Use heading tags to describe your outline. The `<h1>` tag is an example of a heading. The heading tags all begin with h followed by a number indicating the strength of the heading. All your main topics should be denoted by level-one headings. Subtopics should be level-two headings (`<h2>`). The heading levels go all the way to h6, but it's unusual to use anything smaller than level 3.

10. Place most of the text into paragraphs. Although HTML doesn't require use of paragraph tags, they're still a very good idea. Place every paragraph inside a `<p></p>` pair. This will make it much easier to manage the look and behavior of your text later.

11. Save your file with the `.html` extension. Be sure to save the file with a `.html` extension. You can then load the file into a browser to see how it looks.

Some of these elements (especially the headings) will tend to have a particular visual style. The default styles are just there as guidelines. Avoid the temptation to pick headings based on their appearance. When you use CSS in Part 5, you'll be able to make any heading look however you want.

Fleshing Out Your Page

If you've used HTML 4 or XHTML, you'll find HTML5 very familiar. Most of your text will go into paragraphs, marked with the <p></p> pair. Larger sections may be enclosed in divisions, using the <div></div> pair. You'll then add various other elements: images, links, lists, tables, and forms. HTML5 adds a few new elements, but for now, stick with the base that works in every browser.

Adding images

Web pages are capable of far more than text. Figure 2-2 shows a page with an embedded image.

Figure 2-2

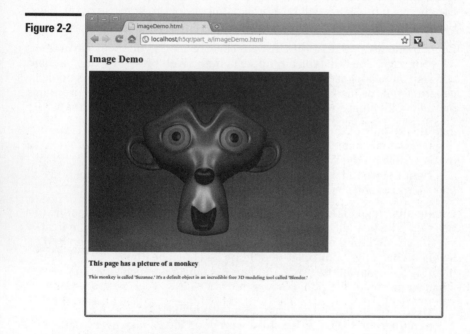

Images are pretty easy to add to Web pages. Here's the code for adding the image:

```
<!DOCTYPE HTML>
<html lang = "en">
<head>
  <title>imageDemo.html</title>
  <meta charset = "UTF-8" />
</head>

<body>
```

```
<h1>Image Demo</h1>

<p>
  <img src = "monkey.png"
       alt = "Picture of a happy monkey" />
</p>
<h2>This page has a picture of a monkey</h2>

<p>
  This monkey is called 'Suzanne.' It's a default
  object in an incredible free 3D modeling tool
  called 'Blender.'
</p>

</body>
</html>
```

Adding an image is relatively easy. Here's what you do:

1. Identify the image you want to use. Of course, you have to have access to an image before you can use it. Be sure you have permission to use the image in your site.

2. Modify the image if necessary. You may need to adjust the image for use on the page. It's best to resize your images before you use them on the Web. You can use commercial image-manipulation software, but I prefer IrfanView or Gimp for this kind of work. Links to both of these free programs are available on my Web site (www.aharrisbooks.net/h5qr/resources.html).

3. Choose your image type. Web browsers can display .jpg, .gif, and .png images. If your image is in another format, use a tool like IrfanView or Gimp to change it to one of these Web-friendly formats.

4. Put your image in the right place. The image file should be in the same directory as the HTML file. That way, when you post your page to the server, it will be easy to move the image as well.

5. Build your page as normal. The image will be placed with a tag embedded into the body.

6. Use the <img> tag to indicate the image. This tag needs to be embedded inside a paragraph or div if you want the page to validate correctly.

7. Use the src attribute to indicate the file containing the image. If the image file is in the same directory as the Web page, all you need is the name of the image. If the image file is elsewhere on the Internet, you can use a complete URL like http://www.aharrisbooks.net/jad/jad_2/monkey.png.

8. Include the `alt` attribute describing the image. The `alt` attribute contains text describing the image. This is important for those who cannot see your image — users with visual impairments, people who have turned off images to increase browsing speed, and search engine bots, which can't see the images but read alt tags.

9. End the image tag with a `/`. The `img` tag is a special tag that doesn't require (or allow) an end tag. The slash character at the end of the tag indicates that the tag is a one-shot tag that serves as its own ending tag.

Including links

The *H* in HTML stands for *hypertext,* which is a fancy term for *links.* Links are one of the things that make the Internet so cool and powerful. It's very easy to add a link to a Web page. Figure 2-3 shows an example with two different kinds of links in it.

Figure 2-3

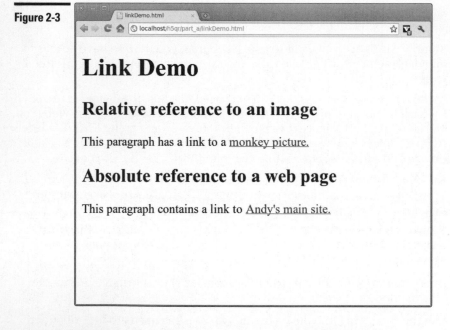

The code for building the links is reproduced here:

```
<!DOCTYPE HTML>
<html lang = "en">
<head>
  <title>linkDemo.html</title>
  <meta charset = "UTF-8" />
</head>
```

```
<body>
  <h1>Link Demo</h1>
  <h2>Relative reference to an image</h2>
  <p>
    This paragraph has a link to a
    <a href = "monkey.png">monkey picture.</a>
  </p>

  <h2>Absolute reference to a web page</h2>
  <p>
    This paragraph contains a link to
    <a href = "http://www.aharrisbooks.net">
      Andy's main site.
    </a>
  </p>

</body>
</html>
```

Links are more than they appear. They display text on the page, but when the user clicks the text, the browser loads a different page on the Internet. Building links into your pages is quite straightforward.

1. Begin with an ordinary page. Links are usually embedded directly into your page. Links cannot stand on their own, but are usually part of some other block-level element like a paragraph.

2. Use the `<a>` tag to indicate a link. The a stands for *anchor.* (I know; it should be the `link` tag, but that term is used for something else in HTML.)

3. Utilize the `href` attribute to describe where the link will go. Most links have an `href` (hypertext reference) attribute, which describes what page should load when the user clicks the link. The href can be a relative or absolute address.

   - *Relative:* The `href` can be a simple filename. If you are linking to a file in the same directory as the Web page you're writing, you can simply indicate the filename. This is known as a *relative reference* because the browser assumes the linked file is in the current directory of the current server. The first link of my example points to the monkey image in the same directory as the page itself.

   - *Absolute:* The `href` can also be a complete Web address. If you prefer, you can give the entire address of a Web site. This is known as an *absolute reference* because it explains how to find the file regardless of the location of the current page. If you want to point to pages or files on somebody else's server, you must use absolute references.

4. Place the visible text between the `<a>` and `</a>` tags. Any text that appears between the `<a>` and the `</a>` tags will be displayed on the screen in a format that indicates a link. The default format is blue underlined text. You find out how to change that (and many other display tricks) in Part 5.

The file you link to can be a Web page or anything else the browser can read. The first link on `linkDemo.html` points to an image file, and the second points to a Web page. Most links point to Web sites, but you can also link anything the browser can read, including images.

Making lists and tables

Pages are often about data, and data is often organized into lists. Figure 2-4 illustrates a page with a series of lists on it.

Figure 2-4

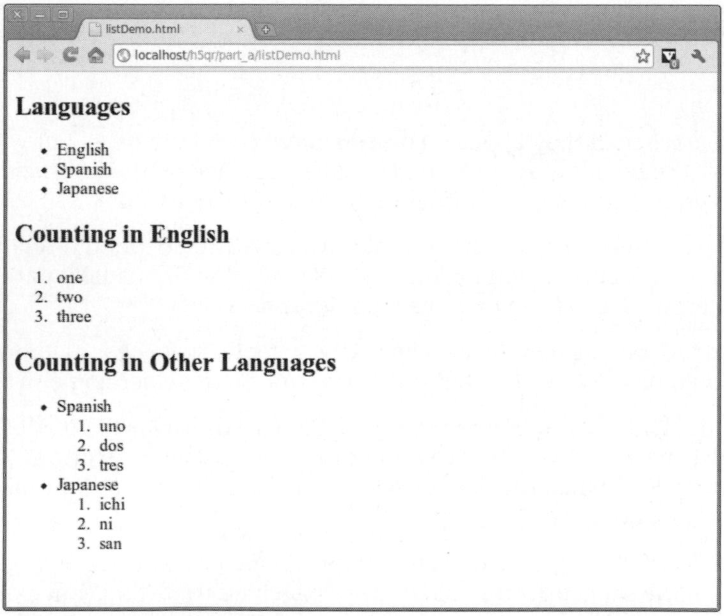

The page in Figure 2-4 shows two main types of lists and a combination list that nests one type into another. Here's the code used to create the lists:

```
<!DOCTYPE HTML>
<html lang = "en">
<head>
  <title>listDemo.html</title>
  <meta charset = "UTF-8" />
</head>
```

```
<body>
  <h2>Languages</h2>
  <ul>
    <li>English</li>
    <li>Spanish</li>
    <li>Japanese</li>
  </ul>

  <h2>Counting in English</h2>
  <ol>
    <li>one</li>
    <li>two</li>
    <li>three</li>
  </ol>

  <h2>Counting in Other Languages</h2>
  <ul>
    <li>Spanish
      <ol>
        <li>uno</li>
        <li>dos</li>
        <li>tres</li>
      </ol>
    </li>

    <li>Japanese
      <ol>
        <li>ichi</li>
        <li>ni</li>
        <li>san</li>
      </ol>
    </li>
  </ul>

</body>
</html>
```

Lists, like most HTML elements, are quite easy to build.

1. Designate the beginning of the list with `<ul>` or `<ol>`. The `<ul>` tag indicates an unordered (bullet) list, and the `<ol>` tag is used to describe an ordered (numbered) list. When you use CSS (described in Part 5) to style your lists, you can have many different kinds of marking, including numbers, Roman numerals, bullets, or custom graphics.

2. Mark each item with an `<li></li>` pair. The `<li>` tag is used to indicate a list item. All elements of a list should be enclosed in the `<li>` tag.

3. (Optional) Nest lists inside each other. The `<li>` of one list can contain an entire new list. This is the technique used to build the nested lists in the example. Just be sure to close off one list before beginning a new one. Proper indentation helps you keep track of how deeply you're nested.

Utilizing tables

Sometimes you will encounter data that is best presented in a tabular format. HTML has a full-featured table system for exactly this purpose. For example, consider the table displayed in Figure 2-5.

Figure 2-5

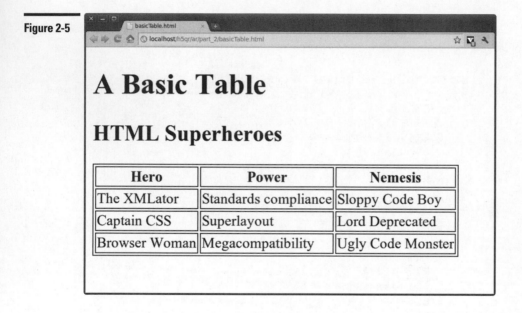

The basic structure of a table in HTML format is reasonably easy to understand. Here's the code that created `basicTable.html`:

```
<!DOCTYPE HTML>
<html lang = "en">
  <head>
    <title>basicTable.html</title>
    <meta charset = "UTF-8" />
    <style type = "text/css">
    table, td, th {
      border: 1px solid black;
```

```
      }
    </style>

  </head>

  <body>
    <h1>A Basic Table</h1>
    <h2>HTML Superheroes</h2>
    <table>
      <tr>
        <th>Hero</th>
        <th>Power</th>
        <th>Nemesis</th>
      </tr>

      <tr>
        <td>The XMLator</td>
        <td>Standards compliance</td>
        <td>Sloppy Code Boy</td>
      </tr>

      <tr>
        <td>Captain CSS</td>
        <td>Superlayout</td>
        <td>Lord Deprecated</td>
      </tr>

      <tr>
        <td>Browser Woman</td>
        <td>Megacompatibility</td>
        <td>Ugly Code Monster</td>
      </tr>

    </table>
  </body>
</html>
```

When you examine this code, you can see that a table is simply a set of carefully nested tags. The process for building a table is not difficult, but it does require some forethought.

1. Plan your table first. It's much easier to build a table in HTML if you already know how it will be structured. You should know how many columns you will have, and which rows or columns will be headlines. It's a good idea to sketch out your table on paper if you're not sure of these things.

2. Begin the table with the `<table>` tag. The `<table></table>` pair encloses the entire table.

3. Create a table row with `<tr>`. The table is defined with a series of rows. Use the `<tr></tr>` pair to enclose each row of data.

4. Signify headings with `<th>`. Some cells will contain headings, and some will contain actual data. Often, the top row will contain headings (sometimes the left-most column will, too). Use the `<th></th>` pair to signify text that should be treated as a heading cell. By default, such cells are generally bolder and centered, but that can be changed with CSS.

5. Specify ordinary data cells with `<td>`. The `<td></td>` pair is used to specify an ordinary data cell. Most of the cells in your table will be specified by `td` tags.

6. Keep the number of cells consistent. Each row should have the same number of cells. (Although there are techniques that allow you to extend a cell across multiple rows or columns, I stick to basic techniques in this introductory part.)

7. Add CSS as needed. Tables do have a basic format, but as usual, you can change things with CSS. I added borders to this example, so it's easier to see the table in Figure 2-5.

8. Do not use tables for layout. The early versions of HTML did not have adequate support for layout (creating columns and precise page layout). Clever HTML developers came up with all sorts of hacks using tables to simulate a layout system. CSS (covered in Parts 5 and 6) provides all the page layout techniques you need, so use of tables should be restricted to its original purpose: presenting tabular data.

Making a Form

From the beginning, Web pages have had the ability to gather data from users. HTML has a standard but quite useful set of form elements that you can use to get input. You can't do anything with the data in plain HTML, but that's what JavaScript and PHP are for. You'll write a number of programs to extract data from Web forms, so it's a good idea to know how they work. Figure 2-6 shows a form containing all the main HTML form elements you might encounter.

Figure 2-6

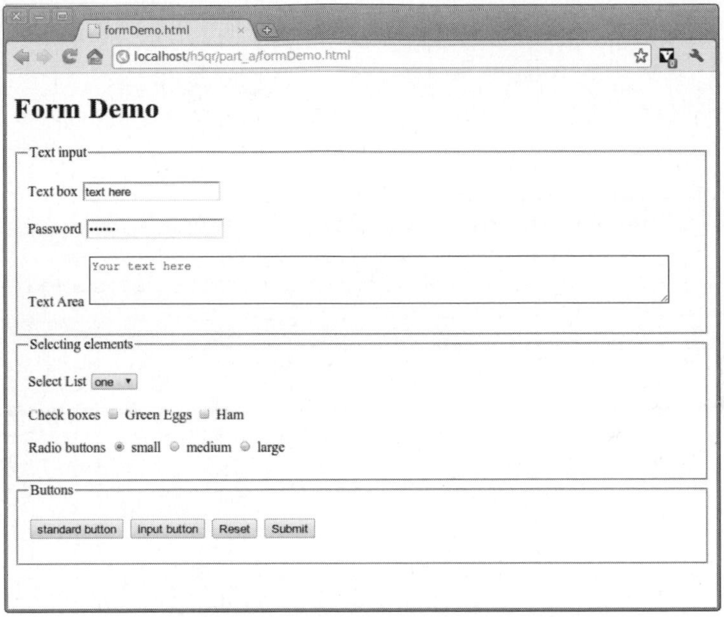

The page in Figure 2-6 has a lot of code on it compared to the earlier examples in this part. I show you the entire code here so you can see how it fits together, and then I explain how the various parts work.

```
<!DOCTYPE HTML>
<html lang = "en">
  <head>
    <title>formDemo.html</title>
    <meta charset = "UTF-8" />
  </head>

  <body>
    <h1>Form Demo</h1>
    <form>
      <fieldset>
        <legend>Text input</legend>
        <p>
          <label>Text box</label>
          <input type = "text"
                 id = "myText"
                 value = "text here" />
        </p>
        <p>
          <label>Password</label>
```

```
      <input type = "password"
             id = "myPwd"
             value = "secret" />
   </p>

   <p>
     <label>Text Area</label>
     <textarea id = "myTextArea"
           rows = "3"
           cols = "80">Your text here</textarea>
   </p>
</fieldset>

<fieldset>
   <legend>Selecting elements</legend>
   <p>
     <label>Select List</label>

     <select id = "myList">
       <option value = "1">one</option>
       <option value = "2">two</option>
       <option value = "3">three</option>
       <option value = "4">four</option>
     </select>
   </p>

   <p>
     <label>Check boxes</label>
      <input type = "checkbox"
             id = "chkEggs"
             value = "greenEggs" />
      <label for = "chkEggs">Green Eggs</label>

     <input type = "checkbox"
             id = "chkHam"
             value = "ham" />
     <label for = "chkHam">Ham</label>
   </p>
   <p>
     <label>Radio buttons</label>
     <input type = "radio"
             name = "radSize"
             id = "sizeSmall"
             value = "small"
             checked = "checked" />
```

```
          <label for = "sizeSmall">small</label>

          <input type = "radio"
                 name = "radSize"
                 id = "sizeMed"
                 value = "medium" />
          <label for = "sizeMed">medium</label>

          <input type = "radio"
                 name = "radSize"
                 id = "sizeLarge"
                 value = "large" />
          <label for = "sizeLarge">large</label>
        </p>
     </fieldset>

     <fieldset>
        <legend>Buttons</legend>
        <p>
          <button type = "button">
            standard button
          </button>

          <input type = "button"
                 value = "input button" />
          <input type = "reset" />
          <input type = "submit" />
        </p>
     </fieldset>
   </form>
 </body>
</html>
```

As you can see, form elements follow many of the same rules as the tags you've already seen, but there are some differences.

The form elements shown in this example are available in all current versions of HTML. *See* Part 4 for information on new form elements available in HTML5.

Form structure tags

These tags are used to help manage the general structure of the form:

  ✔ **<form>:** The <form> tag is the actual tag containing the form. All the form elements are enclosed inside this tag. The <form> tag should also include the action = " " attribute. This indicates that you do not plan to call a server-side script when the form is submitted.

✔ **`<fieldset>`:** This is a special tag that allows you to group a series of input elements together. It is not required, but it can make complex forms easier to navigate. By default, a fieldset has a single border around it, but you can change this with CSS.

✔ **`<legend>`:** A legend can be added to a fieldset. It acts as a label for the entire fieldset.

✔ **`<label>`:** The <label> tag marks text as the label associated with a particular input element. You can use the optional `for` attribute to specify which input element the label is associated with. Label tags are normally used to make CSS styling of forms easier to manage.

The `fieldset`, `legend`, and `label` tags are not required, and frankly, they weren't used much in earlier forms of HTML. These tags are used more commonly in XHTML and HTML5, where use of tables to organize the physical layout of the page is discouraged. These tags help you organize the page so it's easier to lay out with CSS. Proper use of these tags and CSS often makes your forms much easier to work with than the older table-based hacks.

Constructing text input

Many of the form elements are based on the `input` tag. This workhorse is a general-purpose tag used to make a number of interesting input objects. The `type` attribute is used to determine what type of element the tag creates on the page. By far, the most common input element is the basic text box. Its code looks like this:

```
<input type = "text"
       id = "myText"
       value = "text here" />
```

Building it is straightforward.

1. **Create an input element.** The <input> tag creates the general structure of the element.

2. **Set the type to "text".** This indicates you are building a standard text element, not something more elaborate.

3. **Add an `id` attribute.** The `id` attribute allows you to name the element. This will be very important when you add JavaScript to the page because your JavaScript code will use the ID to extract data from the form.

4. **Add default data.** You can add default data if you want, using the `value` attribute. Any text you place in the `value` will become the default value of the form.

The text element will place a small box on the screen. When the user selects the box, the cursor will change to an I-beam, and the user will be able to type text into the box.

Of course, if you want to do something with this text, you'll need to write some code. *See* Bonus Part 1 for information on using JavaScript to read data from forms.

Creating password fields

The standard input element has a cousin that is sometimes used — password. The code for the password looks a lot like the code for a standard input element.

```
<input type = "password"
        id = "myPwd"
        value = "secret" />
```

The password field looks very similar to the ordinary text field, but it does have one primary difference. When the user types data into the text field, the actual contents of the field are replaced by asterisks. This prevents evil henchmen from looking over your shoulders to discover your password.

The password field doesn't provide any real security to speak of. When it is used to send a request to a Web server, that request is normally sent in the clear, where those evil henchmen are sure to find it. In JavaScript processing, the situation is even worse because the code used to retrieve the data will be freely available to the browser. JavaScript is not the language to use if you want to keep a lot of secrets.

Erecting a multiline text box

Sometimes you'll need the ability to enter several lines of text. The text area element is perfect for this situation. Its syntax is a bit different from the `input` element you've seen so far:

```
<textarea id = "myTextArea"
          rows = "3"
          cols = "80">Your text here</textarea>
```

To make your own text area:

1. Begin with the `<textarea>` tag. This tag indicates the beginning of a multiline text box.

2. Specify the number of rows. Indicate the number of rows (or lines) of text you want the text area to contain. Larger boxes accommodate more text but require more room on the screen.

3. Indicate the number of columns. The number of columns shows how wide (in characters) the text box should be. 80 characters is typical for a page-width form.

Forming drop-down lists

Drop-down lists are a common feature in Web pages. They are nice because they allow the programmer to specify a number of choices. The user can choose a selection without typing. Drop-down lists are especially nice because they don't require a lot of screen real estate — the options are visible only while the user is selecting them.

Drop-down lists have one more incredibly important attribute; they prevent certain kinds of errors. The limited options make the response very predictable. When you allow the user to type information into a form, it can be very difficult to check for all the crazy things the user might enter. With a list box, you've already predetermined all the possible answers. There's a lot less that can go wrong.

In HTML/XHTML, drop-down lists are created by two types of object. The overall structure uses the <select> tags, while each of the possible choices has its own <option> tag. Here's how it works:

```
<select id = "myList">
  <option value = "1">one</option>
  <option value = "2">two</option>
  <option value = "3">three</option>
  <option value = "4">four</option>
</select>
```

The select list is a real powerhouse, so you should know how to make it:

1. Create the <select> element first. The container for the list will be a <select> element. The entire list is encased in the <select></select> pair.

2. Give the select element an ID. You'll use this ID to refer to the element in code.

3. Add an option element to the select element. I normally indent the options to remind myself they are part of the select object.

4. Give each option a value. The value will be the response sent to a program when the user chooses an option. The user will not necessarily see the value.

5. Indicate the text the user will see. The text that the user will see for the option goes between the <option> and </option> tags. This can be different from the value, or the same. (That will make more sense after you do some JavaScript coding.)

6. Add as many options as you want. Create a new option object for each choice you want to have available in the list.

TIP

Select boxes don't *have* to have the drop-down behavior. If you want the box to take up more vertical space on the page, just specify the number of rows with the size attribute.

Making checkboxes

Sometimes you'll have some kind of information that can be true or false. The
checkbox element is perfect for this kind of input because the user can click to
select or deselect the option. Checkboxes are another variant of the versatile
input tag:

```
<p>
  <label>Check boxes</label>
   <input type = "checkbox"
          id = "chkEggs"
          value = "greenEggs" />
   <label for = "chkEggs">Green Eggs</label>

   <input type = "checkbox"
          id = "chkHam"
          value = "ham" />
   <label for = "chkHam">Ham</label>
</p>
```

When you build a checkbox, you'll typically also attach a label to the text box.
This way, the user can click the checkbox or the associated label to make a
selection. Checkboxes often appear in groups, but they are independent of each
other. Here's how to build a checkbox:

1. Begin with an input element. Checkboxes are just another form of the
   input element.

2. Set the type attribute to checkbox. This clarifies that the input element
   will be a checkbox. A small checkable box will be placed on the screen.

3. Give the element an id. Like all form elements, you'll need an id field so
   that your code can work directly with the element.

4. Specify a value. You can attach a value to a checkbox. The user won't see
   the value (unless you choose to make the label look just like the value).

5. Add a label. Checkboxes really need to have a label associated with them
   so that the user will understand what the checkbox is about. The label of
   a checkbox is usually applied to the right of the checkbox.

6. Add the for attribute to the label. The label has a special attribute called
   for, which allows you to specify which input element the label corre-
   sponds to. Place the id value of the checkbox into this attribute of the
   label. This is especially useful for checkboxes because in most browsers
   the user can click either the label or the checkbox to trigger the selection.
   Associating the label to the checkbox gives the user a larger target to click
   on, and makes the form easier to use.

HTML forms don't do anything on their own. You'll need to add some sort of programming in JavaScript or HTML to make the form do something.

Popping in radio buttons

On the surface, radio buttons seem a lot like checkboxes, but they are different in a number of important ways.

- **Radio buttons occur only in groups.** You can have one checkbox on a form, but radio buttons make sense only when they are placed in groups.

- **One element of a radio group is selected.** In a radio button group, selecting one button deselects the others. It's like a car radio, where clicking one of the preset buttons deselects the others. (It's really like the old car radios where if the selected station was physically pushed in, the others would pop out. I'm not going to mention that, though, because it would make me seem old.)

- **There should always be one element selected.** When you build a radio group, you should always make one element of the group selected. If not, any programs attached to your form will get confused.

- **The `id` of each radio button is still unique.** Each `id` on a Web page must be unique, and the `id` elements of each radio button will follow the same rules as usual.

- **Each radio element also has a `name` attribute.** The `name` attribute is used to specify the entire *group* of radio objects.

- **All radio buttons in a group have the same name.** HTML uses the `name` attribute to figure out which group a radio button is in, and to ensure that only one button in a group is selected.

Building a radio group is quite similar to creating checkboxes, but there are a few differences.

1. Begin by creating an `input` element. As usual, the `input` element provides the basic foundation.

2. Set the `type` to `radio`. Use the `type` attribute to form radio buttons.

3. Give each element a unique `id`. As usual, apply a unique `id` to each radio button.

4. Give all buttons in a group the same `name`. Use the `name` attribute to identify the buttons in a group.

5. Consider visual grouping as well. The user won't be able to tell which buttons are part of a group by the HTML formatting alone. It might be best to use fieldsets or other formatting tricks to help the user know which buttons are in which group. All buttons in one group should be physically near each other.

6. Make one of the buttons checked (selected) by default. Apply the `checked = "checked"` attribute (provided by the department of redundancy department) to one of the elements so it will start out checked.

Putting in action buttons

One more critical form element is the ubiquitous button. Buttons are great because they just sit there looking irresistible. Users normally expect something important to happen when they click a button. There are actually three main types of buttons, although they all look identical to the user.

- ✔ **Standard button:** A standard button just looks like a button. These buttons are usually used in JavaScript programming to trigger some kind of action on the client end. You use this type of button a lot in JavaScript.

- ✔ **Submit button:** This button is normally used in server-side programming. It packages up all the data in the form and submits it to a program that lives on a remote Web server.

- ✔ **Reset button:** This special button type has built-in behavior. When the user clicks a reset button, all the data in the form is reset to its original default values.

In addition to the three types of buttons, button elements can be created in two different ways. The amazing `input` element can be used to build a button as well, like this:

```
<input type = "button"
       value = "input button" />
```

When used in this way, the `value` property becomes the label of the button, and the `type` property indicates which type of button you intend to build. It isn't necessary to add a label to a button because the label is implied.

This is the original way buttons were created in HTML, and it's still commonly used. But buttons aren't really used for input; they're used to specify that the user wants to do something. For that reason, a new button syntax has evolved:

```
<button type = "button">
   standard button
</button>
```

This syntax introduces a `button` tag with start and end tags. The `type` attribute is used to indicate which type of button you want to use. (The default type is "submit," used primarily in server-side development, which is not the focus of this book.) The text inside the button indicates the text printed on the button. I tend to use the `button` syntax because I think it's cleaner, and also because it makes CSS formatting (see Part 5) a bit easier, as buttons are rarely formatted in the same way as other input elements.

Validating Your Pages

The guidelines described in this part will generally give you a decent Web site, but if you're like me, you'll still make sloppy mistakes sometimes. It would be great if you had some sort of tool that acted like a spell-checker for code. It could look for dumb mistakes like missing tags and stuff that's out of order. Sometimes you'll have junk like that in your code, and you won't even know it's a problem. It may look fine on your browser, but mistakes like this have a habit of appearing when you're hooked up to a projector showing hundreds of people how to build Web sites. (Well, maybe that's just me. . . .)

Fortunately, there is exactly such a code-checker available. The W3 consortium (the same guys who came up with the standards in the first place) have provided a software tool that allows you to check any page to see if it complies with the standards you've declared in the doctype. This tool is called the W3 validator, and it's available at this cleverly named address:

```
http://validator.w3.org
```

Figure 2-7 shows a page being checked by the W3 validator.

The validator is great, but it's not perfect. It can't find every mistake, and of course it works only when you're connected to the Internet. More troubling, the error messages it gives you are sometimes very mysterious and not very helpful.

TIP The W3 validator checks XHTML and HTML5 code. As HTML5 becomes more common, watch for other tools to be available directly in your browser and editor to simplify validating HTML5 code.

Figure 2-7

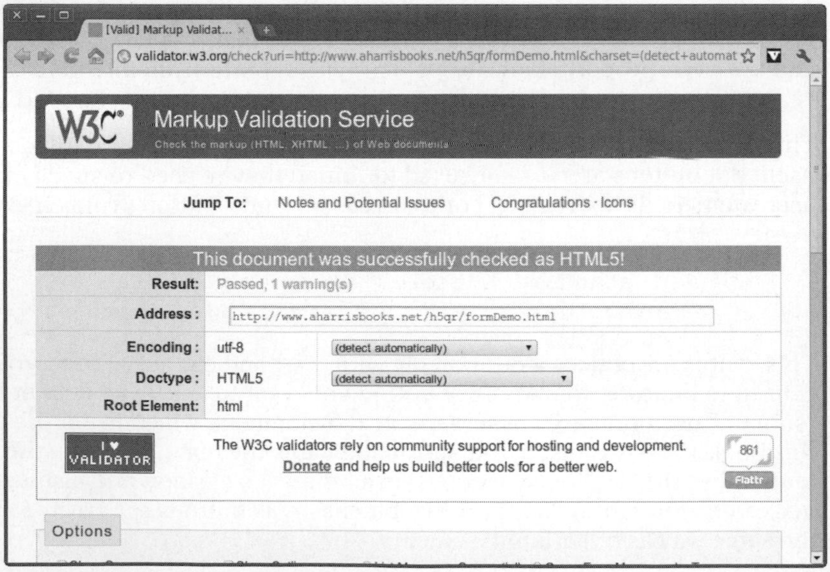

Part 3

New or Changed HTML5 Elements

The interesting thing about having a new version of HTML is the new tags. HTML5 introduces a number of new tags. In addition, a few old friends have new variations. This part takes a look at the new tags and also discusses how some of the old tags have changed.

Be sure to check out my Web site for working examples of every code fragment in the book: www.aharrisbooks.net/h5qr.

In this part . . .

- ✔ **Getting Familiar with Semantic Page Elements**
- ✔ **Taking a Look at Inline Semantic Elements**
- ✔ **Reviewing the Much-Anticipated Media Elements**
- ✔ **Understanding Ruby Elements**

Semantic Page Elements

HTML5 reinforces the notion of semantic markup. That is, tags are not supposed to describe how a section of the page *looks*, but instead should describe the *meaning* of the section in the page context. As Web developers began to embrace these changes in XHTML, pages were full of `<div class = "x">` markups. The semantic page elements added in XHTML are meant to add first-class tags to a few elements common on every page.

<Tip>Firefox 3 supports most of the semantic tags (`header`, `article`, `footer`, and so on) but it displays them as inline elements. Add `display:block` to these elements in CSS, and they'll appear as expected (although they'll still need more CSS to do anything special).

address

The `<address>` tag is intended to hold contact information for the author of a page or section. Although it was available in HTML 4, the `<address>` tag is now intended to be used inside either the entire page content or inside a section or article to indicate the author of that section. Other tags (especially anchors to e-mail addresses or page links) can be embedded in the address.

```
<address>
  10475 Crosspoint Blvd <br />
  Indianapolis, IN 46526
</address>
```

 Most browsers render addresses as italics, but this is not guaranteed. Like any HTML tags, you can modify exactly how the content of the address appears with CSS.

article

An *article* is a subset of the page. The `<article>` tag should be used to indicate content that came from an outside source or is somehow independent of the main page contents. Typically, articles are used to mark sections of the page that are brought in from some sort of aggregation system.

```
<article>
  <header>
  <h1>From
    <em>
      <a href = "http://aharrisboks.net/jad">
        JavaScript and AJAX for Dummies
      </a>
    </em>
  </h1>
```

```
    </header>

    <p>
      Every once in a while, a technology comes along that
      threatens to change everything. AJAX is one such
      technology. In this book, you learn what all the fuss
      is about and why AJAX is such a big deal.
    </p>
  </article>
```

Most browsers do not add any particular formatting to an article; that is up to the CSS definition. Most articles will include a link to the original page if the article is from an online document. The `<article>` tag does not import data from an external source. It only indicates that the relationship is external. For more integrated content, use the `<section>` tag instead. Note that if the article contains a header tag, it is appropriate for the article to have its own h1 heading. This allows page aggregators to pull pages from multiple sources and apply appropriate formatting.

aside

The `<aside>` element is used to indicate a page fragment that is related to but separate from the main content. Aside text is typically formatted as a sidebar.

```
    <aside>
      This is a secondary comment
    </aside>
```

Note that most browsers have not agreed on how to display the aside element (if at all).

footer

The `<footer>` tag is used to represent the footer content of a page. Normally this section contains author contact information (commonly in an `<address>` tag).

```
    <footer>
      <h2>Footer</h2>
      <address>
        Andy Harris <br />
        <a href = "mailto:andy@aharrisbooks.net">
        andy@aharrisbooks.net</a>
      </address>
    </footer>
```

Browsers do not automatically provide style to the footer. Instead, the CSS will determine where the footer actually goes. The `<footer>` tag is mainly intended to replace the `<div id = "footer"></div>` idiom commonly used in HTML 4 and XHTML.

header

The `<header>` tag is primarily used to specify a page header. It replaces the `<div id = "header">` idiom frequently used in HTML 4 and XHTML.

```
<header>
  <h1>This is my header</h1>
</header>
```

The header normally contains an `h1` and other information that belongs in the visual masthead of the page. Do not confuse the `<header>` element (which is a visible section of the page) with the `<head>` element (which contains metadata not shown to the user). Also note that the `<header>` element does not replace the `<h1>` through `<h6>` elements, but usually contains them.

Most browsers do not provide any default formatting to the header. The Web developer is expected to add any desired formatting through CSS.

The `<header>` element has one more use. It can be used inside a section or article to indicate that an `h1` inside that element is a level-one heading for the element, not for the page. This is useful because a page should have only one level-one element. Many pages are built by aggregators or content management systems, so each article and section can have a level-one heading without conflicting with the page's primary heading.

hgroup

The `<hgroup>` tag is used to combine a heading and one or more subheadings into one logical group. The normal heading structure is intended to serve as an outline for the page. Using an h1 heading with an immediate h2 as a subhead interferes with the outlining capabilities. You can put multiple headings in an `hgroup`, and only the initial heading is considered by automatic outlining tools.

```
<hgroup>
  <h1>History of the world</h1>
  <h2>(without all the icky stuff)</h2>
</hgroup>
```

The `hgroup` does not provide any particular formatting to the header group.

menu

The `<menu>` tag and the associated `<command>` element are used to add various types of menu systems.

```
<menu>
  <command label = "one"
           onclick = "alert('uno')">
  <command label = "two"
           onclick = "alert('dos')">
```

```
    <command label = "three"
              onclick = "alert('tres')">
  </menu>
```

The `<menu>` tag supports a `type` attribute that indicates the menu's behavior:

- ✔ **list:** Present the commands much like a list.

- ✔ **context:** Expected to act like a pop-up menu when the user right-clicks an element.

- ✔ **toolbar:** The commands will be presented as a toolbar.

The `menu` element is designed to contain instances of `<command>`. (*See* the "command" section later in this part for details and attributes of the `command` element.) Additionally, the `menu` element does not have any particular visual display associated with it. None of the major browsers display menus with commands yet. (*See* the "command" section later in this part for a workaround.)

Note that the `menu` element has an entirely different meaning in HTML5 than it did in HTML 4. In HTML 4, the `menu` item was a type of list.

nav

The `<nav>` tag is used to indicate a part of the page set aside for page navigation. This is meant to be a replacement for the `<div id = "nav">` idiom frequently used in HTML 4 and XHTML.

```
  <nav>
    <h2>Navigation</h2>
    <ul>
      <li><a href="#">link a</a></li>
      <li><a href="#">link b</a></li>
      <li><a href="#">link c</a></li>
      <li><a href="#">link d</a></li>
      <li><a href="#">link e</a></li>
    </ul>
  </nav>
```

The `nav` element does not have any default formatting. The Web developer is expected to add CSS to determine how the element will look and where it is placed on the page.

section

A `section` is a generic division of a page. A page or an article can be broken into numerous sections. The `section` element is intended to be more specific than the `<div>` tags currently used in HTML 4 and XHTML markup.

```
<section id = "1">
  <h2>Section 1</h2>
  <p>Section body...</p>
</section>
```

So far, there is very little support for the <section> tag among modern browsers. The <article> tag or the standard <div> tag are suitable replacements until browsers begin supporting the section element. Use the detect script described in Part 1 to see if your browser supports this or any other tag before you try to use it.

Inline Semantic Elements

In addition to the page-level semantic element (which adds structure to the entire page), a number of other new or modified tags are intended to add new elements inside a page.

command

The <command> tag is used in the context of the <menu> tag to add a menu system to a page. It can also be used outside of the <menu> tag anywhere on the page to define a keyboard shortcut.

```
<menu>
  <command label = "one"
           onclick = "alert('uno')">
  <command label = "two"
           onclick = "alert('dos')">
  <command label = "three"
           onclick = "alert('tres')">
</menu>
```

The <command> tag accepts a number of attributes:

- **icon:** Indicates the address of an image that will serve as an icon for this command.

- **checked:** Shows if the current command is checked (makes sense only for checkbox and radio commands).

- **disabled:** If this attribute is present, the command is disabled.

- **label:** Identifies the text that will be displayed to the user.

- **onclick:** Indicates a single line of JavaScript code to execute when the user clicks the command.

- ✔ **title:** Displays a tip to the user about what the command does.

- ✔ **type:** Determines the type or behavior of the element. (This can be `command`, `checkbox`, or `radio`.) The types correspond to the same types in ordinary form `input` elements.

At present, no major browsers support the `<command>` tag. However, since the `onclick` attribute can now be attached to nearly any HTML element, you can simulate a list-style menu with the following code:

```
<menu>
  <li onclick = "alert('a')">alpha</li>
  <li onclick = "alert('b')">beta</li>
  <li onclick = "alert('g')">gamma</li>
</menu>
```

While the preceding code is the old HTML 4 interpretation of the menu list, it still validates as HTML5.

Of course, you'll probably want to use CSS to style the list items so they look more like buttons or something clickable.

details

The details element can contain a summary element and other HTML tag. By default, only the summary is visible. When the user activates the details by clicking on the summary, the rest of the content in the details element is displayed. This allows a convenient way to hide and show content.

dfn

The `<dfn>` tag represents a term being defined. Surround the term to be defined with the `<dfn></dfn>` tags.

```
<p><dfn>flollop:</dfn>
  The sound a mattress makes when falling into
  a swamp. <br />
-- Douglas Adams
</p>
```

Most browsers format the `<dfn>` tag as italics, but this can be changed through CSS. The `dfn` element does not replace the *definition list,* which is still used for many types of name-value pairs (although it was designed originally for definitions).

figcaption

The `<figcaption>` tag provides a caption for a figure and should be contained inside only a `<figure>` tag. *See* "figure," next in this part, for more information.

figure

A `figure` is a semantic element that describes one or more images with an optional caption. The `<figure>` tag does not directly display any images; it's meant as a container for holding any type of image (including the standard `<img>` tag but could also include SVG or canvas images). The image can be supplied with an optional caption using the `<figcaption>` tag.

```
<figure>
  <img src = "apoyo.jpg"
       alt = "laguna apoyo" />
  <figcaption>Laguna De Apoyo, Nicaragua</figcaption>
</figure>
```

You can put more than one image inside a figure.

So far, browsers do not provide any particular style or formatting for figures and captions, but these items can be styled through CSS.

summary/details

The `summary` tag is intended to work along with the `details` tag to provide a summary element visible to the user. When the user clicks the summary, all other content in the details element, which was previously hidden, becomes available.

```
<details>
  <summary>Batman's secret identity</summary>
  <p>Bruce Wayne</p>
</details>
```

Note that no major browsers yet support the summary/details combination. Both the summary and the details will be displayed. You can simulate the expected behavior through CSS and JavaScript code.

time

The `time` element provides a field for representing a date or time. This field will contain a date, a time, or a date and a time.

```
<p>
  The rooster crows at <time>6:30</time>
  every morning.
</p>
```

Browsers do not currently apply any special formatting to `time` elements. Data encoded in `time` elements should be formatted in a standard way so they can be adjusted for time zones.

wbr

The `wbr` element is used to add suggestions for word breaks. Put this tag inside a long word to indicate the appropriate place to break the word for word wrap purposes.

```
<p>
  The wbr tag is used to mark a space in a long word
  where it would be ap<wbr>propriate to break the
  word if necessary.
</p>
```

No current browsers support this tag yet.

Media Elements

Perhaps no feature of HTML5 is more anticipated than the media elements. At long last, HTML supports audio and video without an external plugin. Equally exciting is the support for vector-based graphics through the `canvas` and `svg` mechanisms.

audio

The `<audio>` tag allows the user to embed an audio file directly into the browser.

```
<audio src = "DoYou.ogg" controls>
  <a href = "DoYou.ogg">DoYou.ogg</a>
</audio>
```

If the browser does not support the `<audio>` tag, the code between `<audio>` and `</audio>` will be presented instead, so you can provide an ordinary link to let the user download the audio. Or you can embed a Flash player for older browsers.

The `<audio>` tag supports several standard attributes:

✔ **autoplay:** If this attribute is present, the audio file will play immediately when the browser loads the page. Generally this option should not be used, as it's considered rude to play audio without the user's explicit permission.

✔ **controls:** If this attribute is present, the browser will present a simple control interface including play/pause, volume control, and some sort of position indicator. Browsers differ on exactly how the controls appear. It's preferable to give the user some sort of control either through the built-in control mechanism or JavaScript code.

✔ **preload:** If this attribute is present, the audio file will begin to load in memory as soon as the page is loaded, but it will not play until the user activates the player. This can prevent the buffering that might occur if the audio is not preloaded.

✔ **src:** Indicates the address of the file. Note that the `<source>` tag is preferred, as it allows for multiple options.

The `<audio>` tag is supported in some way by all major browsers, and it's expected to be supported in Internet Explorer 9 (IE9). However, the actual audio file formats are not codified in the standard, so different browsers (naturally) support different formats. Most browsers support the open source Ogg standard, but a few (notably Safari and IE9) prefer Mp3. If you supply a version of each, it's likely that any late-model browser will support your audio. Use the `<source>` tag to include multiple audio sources:

```
<audio>
  <source src = "DoYou.ogg">
  <source src = "DoYou.mp3">
</audio>
```

Note that the `audio` element can be controlled through JavaScript code. The following code (invoked in `body.onload`) adds a song element to the page without displaying the audio element:

```
var song;

function init(){
  song = document.createElement('audio');
  song.setAttribute('src', 'DoYou.ogg');
} // end init
```

The code creates an element called `song` and preloads an Ogg file into that song. The following HTML code creates a play button:

```
<button type = "button"
        onclick = "song.play()">
  play
</button>
```

Of course, this button can be styled in any way you want to create your own interface. Once you have an audio element identified in your page, you can apply the following JavaScript functions to it:

✔ **play:** As you might guess, this plays the file. Surprisingly, there is no stop command. You'll either need to pause or set the volume to zero.

✔ **pause:** This pauses the sound. The next play command begins at this spot.

✔ **setAttribute:** This function allows you to modify any of the attributes you would normally set on the HTML `<audio>` tag. This is mainly used to attach a `src` to the audio element.

You can also access a number of useful properties:

- ✔ **currentTime:** This indicates where (in seconds) the song is currently playing. You can read it to find the current position, or set it to cue to a particular part of your song.

- ✔ **volume:** The volume goes from 0 (silent) to 100 (maximum.) You can set or retrieve this attribute through JavaScript code.

canvas

The <canvas> tag sets up a portion of the screen for program-controlled graphics. The HTML simply sets aside a portion of the screen to be used as a canvas. All the drawing and manipulation of the image is done through JavaScript code. The following HTML code sets up a canvas element and provides a button.

```
<canvas id = "myCanvas"
        width = "300"
        height = "200">
  This example requires HTML5 canvas support
</canvas>

<button type = "button"
        onclick = "draw()">
  click me to see a drawing
</button>
```

The canvas element does little on its own. To do anything interesting with the canvas tag, use JavaScript to extract a *drawing context* (a special element that can be drawn on) and use the methods of that context object to create dynamic graphics. For example, here is the draw() function that will be enabled when the user clicks the button:

```
function draw(){
  var myCanvas = document.getElementById("myCanvas");
  var context = myCanvas.getContext("2d");
  context.fillStyle = "blue";
  context.strokeStyle = "red";
  circle(context, 1, 1, 1);

  for (i = 1; i <= 200; i+= 2){
    circle(context, i, i, i, "blue");
    circle(context, 300-i, 200-i, i, "red");
    circle(context, 300-i, i, i, "blue");
    circle(context, i, 200-i, i, "red");
```

```
    } // end for

  } // end draw

  function circle(context, x, y, radius, color){
    context.strokeStyle = color;
    context.beginPath();
    context.arc(x, y, radius, 0, Math.PI * 2, true);
    context.stroke();
  } // end circle
```

The output of the preceding canvas example code is shown in Figure 3-1.

Figure 3-1

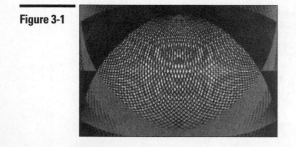

Most modern browsers support some form of the canvas tag directly. IE currently does not support the canvas tag, but you can use the `ExplorerCanvas` plugin to add canvas functionality to IE. IThe IE9 beta appears to support the canvas tag, so this may soon be a universal element.

At the moment, there is only a 2D drawing context available, but support is eventually planned for a 3D drawing context that will allow 3D graphics directly in the browser.

The `context` object controls all the actual drawing functionality. Here are a few of the main methods of the `context` object:

- ✔ **arc():** The arc command draws an *arc* (portion of a circle) as part of a path. The arc is defined like a circle, with a center and radius, but also with beginning and ending angles. If the angles describe a full circle (0 to 2 × pi radians), the arc command will draw a full circle. See the preceding example for a custom circle function created from the arc command.

- ✔ **beginPath():** This command begins the definition of a path. Normally a path is defined by a single moveTo command, followed by a series of lineTo commands, and finished by a stroke, closePath, or fill.

- ✔ **closePath():** This command connects the last point of a path (drawn with moveTo and lineTo commands) to the first, creating a closed shape that can be filled.

✔ **drawImage():** The drawImage command allows you to draw an image (from an external image file) on the canvas. Many implementations allow pixel-level manipulation, allowing you to apply custom filters and transformations to your images, which allows far more control than the typical <img> tag.

✔ **fill():** The fill command (and its variants — like fillRect) allows you to apply the current fill style to elements drawn on the screen.

✔ **fillRect():** This command builds a rectangle of a specified size and position, filled in with the current fill style.

✔ **fillStyle():** Allows you to specify the fill style. This can be a standard color value, or a predefined gradient.

✔ **lineTo():** This command (along with the moveTo command) allows you to build a path on the screen. The lineTo command takes a point as input and draws from a previously defined point to the current point. Note that the path is not displayed until the application of the stroke function.

✔ **lineWidth():** This defines the width of the line being drawn by a stroke command.

✔ **moveTo:** Used in path definition, the moveTo command is used to indicate the starting point of a path.

✔ **stroke():** This command draws the currently defined path. Note that paths are not immediately drawn; the stroke command actually draws the path on the screen.

✔ **strokeRect():** This command draws an unfilled rectangle.

✔ **strokeStyle():** Determines the style of the next stroke to be drawn. Most drawing contexts support dotted and dashed stroke styles, but more are expected.

✔ **text:** Some implementations of the canvas tag allow for text manipulation. This support is uneven, but it is likely to become common in future implementations.

The canvas tag is one of the most important new features of HTML5, as it allows nearly unlimited control of the visual interface. Game developers have begun creating online games using the canvas, and it has already become the basis of several innovative user interface experiments (notably Google maps.)

For more information on programming the canvas element, *see* Part 8 and also check out http://dev.w3.org/html5/canvas-api/canvas-2d-api.html.

embed

The <embed> tag is a universal media tag, so to speak. It can (theoretically, at least) be used to embed any kind of media into the page, specifying the type of media that is to be displayed.

```
<embed src = "monsterTraffic.swf"
       type = "application/x-shockwave-flash"
       width = "400"
       height = "400" />
```

This tag allows you to embed media that isn't supported with other media tags. It uses the `type` attribute to determine the appropriate plugin to use based on MIME type. However, there's no guarantee that the type will be supported. Even if it is, the particular plugin used to display the element is controlled by the client.

The `<embed>` tag was actually removed from HTML and XHTML because it was so unreliable, but it was placed back into use in HTML5. Use `embed` only as a backup to a more reliable tool like the `img`, `audio`, or `video` tags.

The `embed` element is still the best option for including Flash elements, particularly as a backup to the audio or video elements.

source

The `source` tag is used inside an `audio` or `video` element to indicate the source of a media element. Multiple `sources` can be listed. The browser will try each source in order until it finds one it can use. This is the preferred way to indicate multiple possible encodings in an audio or video element. *See* the "audio" section earlier in this part for an example.

svg

The `<svg>` element allows the author to build a vector-based image directly in the page using the SVG markup language.

```
<svg xmlns:xlink="http://www.w3.org/1999/xlink"
xmlns="http://www.w3.org/2000/svg"
viewBox="0 0 200 100"
width="200px" height="100px">

<circle cx="50" cy="50" r="30"
        style="stroke:#0000ff; stroke-width: 5px;
fill:#ff0000;"/>

<rect x = "100"
      y = "0"
      height = "50"
      width = "50"
      stroke-width = "2px"
      stroke = "#ffff00"
      fill = "#00ff00" />

</svg>
```

The output of the svg.html example code here is shown in Figure 3-2.

Figure 3-2

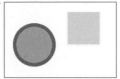

SVG uses an XML system very similar to XHTML. Each element is described by a tag, which has various attributes defining its size, position, and color. SVG elements can also be modified by a form of CSS. It's also possible to use JavaScript code to create and modify SVG code in real time. SVG is often used to create charts or other visualizations dynamically. Also, it's possible to export an SVG image from a tool like Dia or Inkscape, and embed the resulting drawing directly in the page.

The main advantage of a vector-based image format like SVG is the ability to scale the image without losing image quality.

All major browsers except IE already support some level of SVG in the most current release, and Microsoft plans to include SVG in IE9.

For more information on the SVG standard, please see the W3C SVG page at www.w3.org/Graphics/SVG.

video

The video element is one of the more anticipated features of HTML5. With this tag, developers will be able to embed videos into a Web page without requiring a plugin like Flash.

```
<video src = "bigBuck.ogv" controls>
   Your browser does not support embedded video
   through HTML5.
</video>
```

The <video> tag itself is pretty simple to understand, but the actual implementation is somewhat complex. HTML5 indicates a video tag, but it doesn't specify what format the browser will support. It will not surprise you that all the browser manufacturers have a different opinion about which format will be supported. At the moment, there are three main video formats in contention.

 ✔ **Ogg/Theora/Vorbis:** Ogg is a container format which uses Vorbis encoding for audio and Theora encoding for video. The Ogg system is unencumbered by any known patents. It's supported by Firefox, Chrome, and Opera. (It's also supported by Safari if the user has installed the Vorbis plugin to QuickTime.) IE9 doesn't plan to support this format at all.

✔ **MP4/H.264/AAC:** The MP4 standard is a container format using H.264 for video encoding and AAC for audio encoding. All three formats are subject to patent restrictions. This format is supported by Safari, Chrome, iPhone, and Android. IE plans to support it in IE9.

✔ **WebM/VP8/Vorbis:** WebM is a relatively new standard introduced by Google. It uses the VP8 video encoding format and Vorbis audio encoding. There's little support for WebM yet, but most browsers are indicating support for the format in upcoming versions.

If you want to incorporate HTML5 video, use the <source> tag to include all the major formats. (You can use the free FFmpeg tool available for all major software platforms to convert your videos.) As a final fallback, use the <embed> tag inside your <video> tag to load the video with a Flash player.

You can use JavaScript to control the video element in the same way you control audio. *See* the "audio" section earlier in this part for more information about controlling your media elements through JavaScript code.

Ruby Elements

The Web is a truly international phenomenon. HTML5 acknowledges this phenomenon with a series of tags that support *Ruby,* a form of markup used primarily with Asian languages.

 Note that Ruby is also the name of a programming language (which originated in Japan) sometimes used in server-side Web development. In the context of HTML5, Ruby refers to the markup mechanism, not the programming language.

ruby

The <ruby> tag marks a segment of code that is expected to include Ruby annotations.

rt

The <rt> tag is placed inside Ruby markup. It contains a pronunciation guide to the preceding character. It's primarily used for rarely-used characters in languages such as Chinese and Japanese.

rp

Officially, the <rp> tag is used when the browser does not support <rt>.

At the moment, no major browsers support any of the Ruby markups.

Part 4

New and Modified Form Elements

Forms have been a part of HTML since the very beginning. As Web sites have morphed into application frameworks, the basic form elements are beginning to show their age. A number of tools (including XForms and third-party add-ons like jQuery UI) have tried to give form elements a face-lift. HTML5 finally adds some much-needed attention to form elements. The standard includes several new form elements as well as a number of additions to the standard input element and new attributes that can be applied to any form element.

In this part . . .

- ✓ **Introducing New Form Elements**
- ✓ **Examining New Form Element Attributes**
- ✓ **Playing with New Form Input Types**

New Form Elements

A number of new form elements have been introduced in HTML5. Each of these new tools adds a new capability. Of course, they're not all supported yet, but they do show some promise. A notable subset of these form elements are designed to let a program modify a part of the page dynamically.

datalist

The datalist element allows the developer to attach a list of suggestions to a text input element. As soon as the user begins to type in the text field, the list of suggestions appears and the user can choose from the suggestions with the mouse.

```
<label for = "txtList">Your name
  <input type = "text"
         list = "names"
         id = "txtList"/>
  <datalist id = "names">
    <option value = "Andy">
    <option value = "Andrew">
    <option value = "Androcles">
  </datalist>
</label>
```

The datalist element is currently supported by Opera only. You can embed an ordinary HTML <select> element (with the same id as the text element) inside the datalist object. Browsers that can support the datalist will do so, and others will display the select element.

A number of other fields (notably the number input type) have a list attribute that connects that element to a datalist. This is intended to allow a datalist to be connected to other kinds of input, but there is little support yet for this behavior.

fieldset

The fieldset element isn't technically new to HTML5, but it's not widely used by developers. All form elements are supposed to be embedded in some sort of block-level element, and the fieldset is the obvious tool for the job. By default, the fieldset draws a simple black border around its child tags. Use the <legend> tag to add a label to the fieldset.

```
<form action = "">
  <fieldset>
    <legend>My Form</legend>
    <label for = "myInput">
      <input type = "text"
             id = "myInput" />
    </label>
```

```
      </fieldset>
    </form>
```

The `fieldset` element is supported in all major browsers.

keygen

The `keygen` element generates an encryption key for passing encrypted data to a server.

```
        <label for = "key">keygen
          <keygen id = "key"
                  keytype = "rsa"
                  challenge = "openSesame" />
        </label>
```

The `<keygen>` tag has a number of parameters:

- ✔ **keytype:** Specifies the type of encryption. (`rsa` is standard.)

- ✔ **challenge:** A string that is passed along with the public key. (This is normally specified by the server.)

The `keygen` element is hotly debated in the HTML5 community. Some security experts consider its encryption mechanism already obsolete, and use of the tool requires knowledge of encryption that a relatively small number of Web developers possess. The `keygen` element isn't currently supported in any browser, and it may not become a part of the standard.

label

Like the `fieldset` element, the `label` has been around for some time but has been underutilized. The `label` tag allows you to attach an HTML element to a form input element. The `for` attribute holds the `id` of the element related to the label. Form elements are often embedded into labels to simplify CSS formatting, and the label can offer some user-interface advantages. For example, if a label is attached to a check box or radio option, the user can click the label or the option to make a choice.

Some Web developers embed an input tag inside the corresponding label for easier CSS formatting. I use that technique throughout this reference.

Use of fieldsets, labels, and some basic CSS eliminates the need to use tables for form layout. The following CSS shows one easy way to make a form line up nicely without adding the extra complexity of tables for layout management:

```
      <style type = "text/css">
        label{
          display: block;
          width: 60%;
```

```
      text-align: right;
      margin-right: 1em;
    }
    input {
      width:40%;
    }
</style>
```

meter

The `meter` tag indicates a numeric value that falls within a range.

```
<p>
A
<meter min = "0"
       max = "10"
       value = "7"></meter>
</p>
```

The `meter` tag can be placed in a form or anywhere else it is desirable to indicate that a value falls within a prescribed range. The `meter` tag supports a number of attributes:

- ✔ **value:** If this is not specified as an attribute, the first numeric value inside the `<meter></meter>` pair will be seen as the value.

- ✔ **max:** The maximum possible value of the item.

- ✔ **min:** The minimum possible value of the item.

- ✔ **high:** If the value can be defined as a range, this is the high end of the range.

- ✔ **low:** If the value can defined as a range, this is the low end of that range.

- ✔ **optimum:** This is the optimal value of the element.

The `value`, `high`, `low`, and `optimum` values should all be between `min` and `max`. No particular display mechanism is indicated for this element, though the webkit-based browsers currently display a small bar graph. Note that the meter element is used to *output* a numeric element. Use `<input type = "range">` for numeric input within a range.

The `meter` tag is often used in a form, but it can occur anywhere in a document. The `value` of the `meter` can be changed dynamically through JavaScript like the `value` of any form element.

output

The `output` element is meant to display text output. It indicates a section of the page that will be modified by a script (usually JavaScript). Consider the following code fragment:

```
<output id = "myOutput">
  This is the original value
</output>
<button onclick = "changeOutput()">
  change the output
</button>
```

When the button is pressed, it will call the `changeOutput()` JavaScript function, which could look like this:

```
function changeOutput(){
  var myOutput = document.getElementById("myOutput");
  myOutput.value = "The value has changed";
} // end changeOutput
```

When this function runs, it changes the content of `myOutput`.

The `output` element is currently supported by Opera. It does not have any particular visual style associated with it.

Until usage of this element becomes more widespread, you can use the `innerHTML` attribute of any page element to change its content dynamically through code.

The `output` tag is often embedded in forms, as it's a user-interaction element, but it can occur anywhere in the page.

progress

The `<progress>` tag indicates how much of a task has been completed (often marked as a percentage).

```
    <p>Now destroying the world. <br />
<p>
  progress:
  <progress value = "25"
            max = "100"></progress>
</p>
```

Most browsers indicate the progress as plain text, but it's reasonable to suppose some sort of visual gauge may become available.

The `progress` element is expected to be modified through JavaScript code. Because it's associated with JavaScript, `progress` elements are often included in forms, but they can be placed anywhere on a page.

New Form Element Attributes

In addition to the new form elements introduced in HTML5, all the form elements got a few new goodies. These new attributes and capabilities can be applied to any form element.

autofocus

The `autofocus` attribute can be applied to any form element. If an element has this attribute, that element will be the focus of the first user input. It's common to apply the `autofocus` attribute to the first element of the form.

```
<form action = "">
  <fieldset>
    <label>name
      <input type = "text"
             autofocus />
    </label>
    <label>email
      <input type = "email">
    </label>
  </fieldset>
</form>
```

If the browser does not accept the `autofocus` attribute, nothing harmful will happen, and you can still use a JavaScript-based solution. Of course, it makes sense to have only one autofocus field per form.

pattern

The `pattern` attribute allows you to specify a regular expression used to validate the form. If the content matches the regular expression, the field will be considered valid. (*See* the "Validation" section later in this part for more details.) The `pattern` attribute should be used only when the standard validation techniques are not sufficient, as it can be difficult to debug regular expressions.

```
<input type = "text"
       id = "txtPhone"
       pattern = "\(\d{3}\) +\d{3}-\d{4}"
       title = "(ddd) ddd-dddd" />
```

When you specify a pattern, you should also include a `title` attribute. The title should indicate what the pattern is. The browser can use this as a tip for the user. It may also be useful to add pattern information as placeholder text. (**See** the next section for more information.)

See Chapter 7 of my book *JavaScript & AJAX For Dummies* (Wiley Publishing) for a complete description of regular expressions and how to use them for page validation.

placeholder

The `placeholder` attribute allows you to add a special placeholder value in your text fields. This placeholder acts as a temporary label showing the purpose of the field without requiring a label tag. As soon as the user activates the field, the placeholder text disappears.

```
<input type = "text"
       placeholder = "Name" />
```

Not all browsers support placeholder text. Other browsers will simply ignore the `placeholder` attribute. Likewise, if the field is already filled in, the place-holder will not be visible. For these reasons, it's still preferred to add a label so users know what to type in each text area. Placeholder text is especially helpful when it's used to indicate how the input should be formatted (especially if this will be enforced by validation or a pattern).

required

The `required` attribute allows you to specify a particular field as required. Supporting browsers will mark all required fields (perhaps by highlighting them in red) if they aren't filled in. Some browsers will also send a warning if the user tries to submit a form with empty required fields.

```
<input type = "text"
       required />
```

The special `:required` pseudo-class allows you to apply a CSS style to all required elements in your form (giving them a border or background color, for example). Here's an example of a CSS style for marking required elements with a red border:

```
:required {
  border: 1px solid red;
}
```

Validation

Form validation is one of the trickiest parts of Web development. It's pretty easy to set up a form that asks for user information, but it can be quite difficult to be certain that the user enters information correctly. For example, an e-mail address should contain a few letters, an "at" (@) symbol, a few more letters, a period, and a top-level domain of two to four characters. Typically programmers use tricks like regular expression parsing in JavaScript to ensure the data is in the right format.

See my book *JavaScript & AJAX For Dummies* (Wiley) for a complete discussion of how to do form validation with regular expressions if you need to support validation without HTML5.

HTML5 promises a much easier solution. When you use the special-purpose input elements (described in the next section), the browser will automatically check the form field to ensure it's in a proper format. If the entry is not valid, the form will (generally) not submit, and the special :invalid CSS pseudo-class will be associated with the invalid field. Simply supply CSS to your page handling the :invalid state:

```
:invalid {
  background-color: red;
}
```

When this CSS state is active, any invalid fields will have the :invalid styling. For example, if you have a color field and the red background CSS style defined here, the color field will have a red background unless the user enters in a valid color (a recognized color name or hex color value). Likewise, the e-mail field will show red until a valid e-mail address is entered.

The developer doesn't need to add any other code to the form. Simply add CSS to display invalid entries, and the browser will do the rest.

Note that if a field is required (with the required attribute), it will be considered invalid until it contains some value.

It's possible that the browser will refuse to process a form until all fields are validated, but this behavior does not yet seem to be universal among HTML5–compliant browsers.

If you want, you can turn off the validation for any field by adding the novalidate attribute to that element.

New Form Input Types

HTML forms are centered around the humble but flexible input element. This same element is used in HTML 4 to build many different types of interface widgets, from standard text and password fields to radio buttons and check boxes. HTML5 adds a number of very useful forms of input, which help turn HTML into a more modern user-interface tool.

Although support for these tags is not universal, it's safe to begin using them now. Any browser (even IE6) which does not understand the advanced input types will revert to `input type = "text"`, which will still work exactly as expected (although not with the validation and user-interface improvements of the newer tags).

Note that the standard indicates that the various types will be supported, but the exact way the elements are supported will vary from browser to browser. For example, the e-mail field will likely look just like an ordinary text field to a user with a standard desktop machine, but the virtual keyboard on a mobile device might change to include the @ when it encounters an e-mail field.

Most of these specialty fields do support validation, so at a minimum, it's useful to set an `:invalid` CSS style so the user can tell if the data is in the field

color

The `color` tool allows the user to choose a color using standard Web formats — recognized color names (yellow) and hex values preceded by a # symbol (#FF0033). The browser may display a color-picking tool like the ones found in word processors and image-editing programs. At the moment, most browsers simply display a text box and indicate whether the current content is a valid color name or value.

```
<input type="color"
       id = "color" />
```

date

Setting the input type to `date` indicates that you want the user to enter a date value. Some browsers (Firefox 3.5) will still display a text field, and others (Opera 10) will display a special calendar control, allowing for much more accurate and easier date selection. Still other browsers (Chrome) will include both text and a pop-up calendar. If the date is entered by text, it must be entered in a yyyy-mm-dd format.

```
<input type="date"
       id = "date" />
```

You can restrict the dates allowed to a specific range by applying the `min` and `max` attributes to the element.

datetime

The `datetime` element combines `date` and `time` into a single element. It also includes a mechanism for entering the time zone.

```
<input type="datetime"
       id = "datetime" />
```

Some browsers will pop up a calendar control for the date and a formatted input for the time. Others may modify virtual keyboards for date and time input.

The official full date and time format returned from the various date and time elements is a specialized code:

```
yyyy-mm-ddThh:mm+ff:gg
```

Each of the characters in the code describes a part of the date and time:

- ✔ **yyyy:** Four digits for the year.

- ✔ **-:** An actual dash character, which must be placed between year and month. Another dash is placed between the month and the day.

- ✔ **mm:** Two digits for the month.

- ✔ **dd:** Two digits for the day.

- ✔ **T:** The capital *T* indicates the beginning of the time part of the code.

- ✔ **hh:** Two digits for the hour, in 24-hour format.

- ✔ **::** The colon character between the hour and minutes. Another colon will appear between the hour and minutes of the time zone offset.

- ✔ **mm:** Two digits for the minutes.

- ✔ **+/-/z:** The time zone offset is indicated by a capital *Z* (if the time is Zulu or GMT time) or the + or - symbol if time is in another time zone.

- ✔ **ff:** If the time zone is not Zulu time, indicate the number of hours offset from GMT.

- ✔ **gg:** Number of minutes offset from Zulu time. Typically this is 00, but it is possible that the time zone will be offset by 15, 30, or 45 minutes.

For example, 5:30 PM on October 11, 2010, in New York City will be indicated like this:

```
2010-10-11T17:30-05:00
```

If the user is using a browser that validates a `dateTime` field, the date and time will need to be in this format to be considered valid. The value of a `dateTime` field will be in this format, which is relatively easy for computer programs to parse and manage.

datetime-local

The `datetime-local` element is just like the `datetime` element except it does not include a time zone indicator.

```
<input type="datetime-local"
       id = "datetimeLocal" />
```

The `datetime-local` input type expects and returns a date and time in the same format as the standard `datetime` element, except `datetime-local` does not include a time zone offset.

email

The `email` element generally looks like a plain text field, but it validates on an e-mail address. Also, it is possible that the browser will modify the user experience in other ways. For example, mobile browsers may modify the virtual keyboard to include the @ symbol, which is always present in e-mail addresses.

```
<input type="email"
       id = "txtEmail" />
```

month

The `month` input type generates a four-digit year followed by a two-digit month. It frequently pops up the same calendar control as other date pickers, but only the year and month (yyyy-mm format) are returned.

```
<input type = "month"
       id = "month" />
```

number

The `number` field allows the input of numerical data. This often consists of a text field followed by some kind of selector (for example, up and down arrows), or it might change the virtual keypad of a portable device to handle only numeric input.

```
<input type = "number"
       id = "number"
       max = "10"
       min = "0" />
```

The `number` input type supports several special attributes:

- **min:** This is the minimum value allowed. If there is an onscreen input element, it will not allow a value less than the `min` value. The field will also not validate if the value of the field is less than the `min` value.

- **max:** This is the maximum allowed value. If there is an onscreen input element, it will not allow a value larger than the `max` value. The field will not validate if the value of the field is larger than the `max` value.

- **step:** This value indicates how much the visual interface tools (typically small up and down arrows) will change the value when activated.

- **value:** This is the numeric value of the element.

All attributes of the number element can be integer or floating point. However, current browsers that support this tag (Opera and Chrome) do not seem to validate as well with floating-point values as they do with integer values. For more control of numeric input, consider the `range` input type. (***See*** the next section.)

range

The `range` input type is a long-anticipated addition to the HTML toolbox. User-interface experts have known for years that user input of integer values is very difficult to get right. Most user-interface toolkits have some sort of slider or scrollbar mechanism, which makes it easy for users to enter a numeric value visually. The `<input type = "range">` construct finally adds this functionality to HTML forms.

```
<input type = "range"
       id = "range"
       min = "0"
       max = "255"
       value = "128" />
```

The `range` input takes the same attributes as `number`, `min`, `max`, `value`, and `step`. If the browser supports the `range` tag, the user will see a scroller; if not, a plain-text input type will appear. When the `range` element becomes widespread, its use will be encouraged because it's much easier to restrict the user's input to a valid range (especially when the mechanism for doing so is visual and easy) than it is to check the user's input after the fact.

However, the `range` type doesn't display the exact value, and it can be harder to get precise results than with the `number` input type. One solution is to pair an `output` tag to the `range`, and use JavaScript to update the output when the range is changed. Here's a sample form that incorporates this idea:

```
<form action = "">
  <fieldset>
    <input id = "myRange"
           type = "range"
           min = "0"
           max = "255"
           value = "128"
           onchange = "updateOutput()" />

    <output id = "myOutput">128</output>
  </fieldset>
</form>
```

When the `range` value is changed, it calls a JavaScript function called `update Output`. Here is that function:

```
function updateOutput(){
  //get elements
  var myRange = document.getElementById("myRange");
  var myOutput = document.getElementById("myOutput");

  //copy the value over
  myOutput.value = myRange.value;
} // end function
```

Like the `number` input type, the `range` can be given floating-point values if preferred.

search

The `search` input type is used to retrieve text that's intended to be used as part of a search (either internally or through some searching service like Google). On most browsers, it's displayed like an ordinary text field. It does sometimes have some special behavior. On Safari, the search field is displayed with a small *x*, which clears the contents of the search. On Chrome, the autocompletion features of the main search bar (which is also the URL input element in Chrome) are automatically applied to the search box.

```
<input type="search"
       id = "search" />
```

Like the other new input types, there's no penalty for using the `search` element in browsers that don't support it. The fallback is a plain-text input.

Note that the `search` element doesn't actually do any searching. If you want to actually search for the value, you'll still need to write some code. The `search` element does give you an interface consistent with the browser's integrated search tools, but the actual behavior is still up to the programmer.

tel

The `tel` field is used to input a telephone number. It expects three digits followed by a dash and four digits. You may need to play with the `pattern` attribute if you want to allow an area code or extensions to validate.

```
<input type = "tel"
       id = "tel"  />
```

time

The purpose of the `time` input type is to allow the user to enter a time. Time is stored in `hh:mm` format, where `hh` is the hour (in 24-hour format), and `mm` is the minutes. Some browsers will include a colon directly in the field, and some will modify the virtual keyboard with numbers and the colon character. It's also possible that a browser will pop up some sort of custom time selector, but this isn't yet supported in any major browsers.

```
<input type = "time"
       id = "time" />
```

url

Use the `url` input type to indicate a Web address. Browsers that support this element will check for the `http://` prefix. Mobile browsers may also adapt the virtual keyboard to include characters commonly found in URLs: the colon (:), forward slash (/), and tilde (~).

```
<input type = "url"
       id = "url"  />
```

week

The `week` field is used to pick a week from a calendar control. It returns a value in the following format:

`yyyy-Wnn`

- ✔ **yyyy:** Represents a four-digit year.

- ✔ **-:** The dash character.

- ✔ **w:** The capital *W* character.

- ✔ **nn:** The week as a two-digit number.

Some browsers will pop up the standard calendar control. When the user selects a date (or a week), only the year and week will be returned. Other browsers will simply validate for the proper format.

```
<input type = "week"
       id = "week" />
```

Part 5

Formatting with CSS

Early forms of HTML paid very little attention to the visual aspects of page layout. The original plan was for HTML to be more tied to the *meaning* of page elements rather than their display. In the very early days of the Web, this was fine, but soon people wanted far more sophisticated design elements than HTML was capable of producing. Browser manufacturers responded by adding vendor-specific tags that added new capabilities but greatly complicated development efforts.

HTML5 is an attempt to return HTML to its earlier simplicity. All the tags that were once used to directly manage the appearance of the page (tags like <font>, <center>, <b>, and <i>) are removed. Rather than having special tags indicate formatting, a new language has been devised that can provide very powerful formatting features to virtually any HTML/XHTML tag. CSS (Cascading Style Sheets) is this language.

This part is a review of CSS as it currently stands. If you're already familiar with CSS technology, feel free to skip this part. However, if you need a review of the current state of the art, you're in the right place. The CSS described here works on all major browsers. Part 6 describes the new CSS features available as part of HTML5.

Be sure to check out my Web site for working examples of every code fragment in the book: www.aharrisbooks.net/h5qr.

In this part . . .

- ✔ **Getting an Overview of CSS**
- ✔ **Controlling the Look of Your Page**
- ✔ **Utilizing Float Positioning**

A Quick Overview of CSS

CSS works by describing certain parts of the page (one particular tag, all the tags of a specific type, or all tags sharing a particular characteristic). For each of these tag groups, you can then identify a number of *rules*. Each rule is a name/value pair. Take a look at the simple page displayed in Figure 5-1.

Figure 5-1

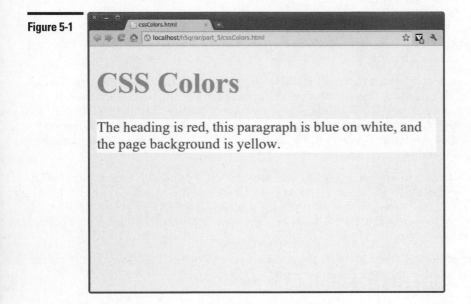

The code to produce this page is shown here:

```
<!DOCTYPE HTML>
<html lang = "en">
<head>
  <title>cssColors.html</title>
  <meta charset = "UTF-8" />
  <style type = "text/css">
    body {
      background-color: yellow;
    }

    h1 {
      color: red;
    }

    p {
      color: blue;
      background-color: white;
```

```
      }
   </style>

</head>
<body>
   <h1>CSS Colors</h1>

   <p>
      The heading is red, this paragraph is blue on white, and
the page background is yellow.
   </p>
</body>
</html>
```

It goes without saying that a page about colors is disappointing to view in a black-and-white book. As always, be sure to look on the book's companion Web page (www.aharrisbooks.net/h5qr) to see this page in full and try it on your own machine.

The new elements are not terribly surprising, but they are quite powerful. Note that the colors are changed without changing anything in the HTML body. All the real action happens in a special part of the header. This is part of the charm of CSS. It makes your HTML a lot cleaner because much of the formatting can go elsewhere. Here's how to add color formatting (or any CSS, for that matter) to your pages:

1. Begin with clean valid HTML code. Be sure your HTML code validates before trying to do too much else with it. Improper HTML won't always respond to CSS the way you think it should.

2. Add a `<style>` tag to the page heading. The `<style>` tag allows you to add a *style sheet* (a list of formatting instructions) directly on the page. *See* "Managing levels of CSS" later in this part for how to put style sheets in other places.

3. Set the style's type to `text/css`.

The only value you'll ever use for style type is `text/css`.

4. Indicate the tag you want to modify. The first tag I change is the body. Changes to the `body` tag will affect the entire visible part of the page, so this is a great place to start. Just type the tag name (without the angle braces).

5. Use squiggly braces ({}) to enclose the rules for this style. You may have several rules to describe how the body should be displayed. For each style, you'll need to enclose all the rules in a pair of braces.

6. Denote the background-color attribute. Every rule consists of an *attribute* and a *value*. The attribute is a built-in characteristic of the element, and the value is the value we want to give that attribute. For now, change the background color of the background, so type `background-color:`. Note that you must end the attribute name with a colon (:). Capitalization and spelling count, so be careful.

7. Indicate the value you want to apply to the attribute. For this example, I want a yellow background, so I just type the value `yellow;` after the attribute `background-color:`. This will cause the body's background color to be set to yellow.

8. End each value with a semicolon(;). Every value must end with a semicolon. If one tag has a lot of rules (which is common) the semicolons help the browser separate all the various rules from each other.

9. Change the foreground color with the `color` attribute. Note how I make the level-1 headline red. Set h1 as the new tag, and set its `color` attribute to the value `red`.

10. One tag can have multiple rules. Take a look at the rules for the paragraph (p) tag. You'll see that I set both the foreground and background colors.

You find more about which colors you can use in the next section. For now, though, just play around with the various color names. Most of the common color names will work just like you expect. When you want a fancier color, you'll have to find out how to use the fancy hex codes; *see* "Comprehending hex colors" later in this part.

Employing local styles

CSS has a rich mechanism for working with colors. Whenever you want to specify a color, you can simply type the color name. Figure 5-2 demonstrates the 16 color names that CSS understands.

Figure 5-2

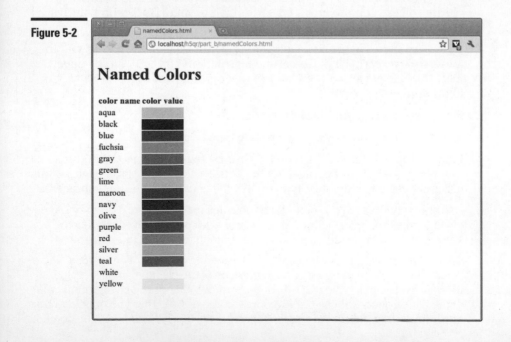

A page that demonstrates colors isn't very useful in a black-and-white book, so you'll definitely want to view this page (and all of the others in this book) on my Web site (www.aharrisbooks.net/h5qr).

The namedColors.html page featured in Figure 5-2 has another trick up its sleeve. Take a look at the source code and you'll see what I mean:

```html
<!DOCTYPE HTML>
<html lang = "en">
<head>
  <title>namedColors.html</title>
  <meta charset = "UTF-8" />
</head>

  <body>
    <h1>Named Colors</h1>
    <table>

      <tr>
        <th>color name</th>
        <th>color value</th>
      </tr>

      <tr>
        <td>aqua</td>
        <td style="background-color: aqua;"><br /></td>
      </tr>

      <tr>
        <td>black</td>
        <td style="background-color: black;"><br /></td>
      </tr>

      <tr>
        <td>blue</td>
        <td style="background-color: blue;"><br /></td>
      </tr>

      <tr>
        <td>fuchsia</td>
        <td style="background-color: fuchsia;"><br /></td>

      </tr>

      <tr>
        <td>gray</td>
        <td style="background-color: gray;"><br /></td>
```

```
  </tr>

  <tr>
    <td>green</td>
    <td style="background-color: green;"><br /></td>
  </tr>

  <tr>
    <td>lime</td>
    <td style="background-color: lime;"><br /></td>
  </tr>

  <tr>
    <td>maroon</td>
    <td style="background-color: maroon;"><br /></td>
  </tr>

  <tr>
    <td>navy</td>
    <td style="background-color: navy;"><br /></td>
  </tr>

  <tr>
    <td>olive</td>
    <td style="background-color: olive;"><br /></td>
  </tr>

  <tr>
    <td>purple</td>
    <td style="background-color: purple;"><br /></td>
  </tr>

  <tr>
    <td>red</td>
    <td style="background-color: red;"><br /></td>
  </tr>

  <tr>
    <td>silver</td>
    <td style="background-color: silver;"><br /></td>
  </tr>

  <tr>
```

```
      <td>teal</td>
      <td style="background-color: teal;"><br /></td>
    </tr>

    <tr>
      <td>white</td>
      <td style="background-color: white;"><br /></td>

    </tr>

    <tr>
      <td>yellow</td>
      <td style="background-color: yellow;"><br /></td>
    </tr>
  </table>
  </body>
</html>
```

This page uses a table to demonstrate all the colors that CSS recognizes. Next to the color name is a table cell with the background color set to that color. Note that in this case, rather than having one large style sheet at the top of the document, I added several smaller styles directly inside the body of the HTML page. This technique is called *local styles*.

Most HTML tags have an attribute called `style`. You can add CSS rules directly to this style if you want. For example, to make the aqua-colored cell, look at the following code:

```
      <td style="background-color: aqua;"><br /></td>
```

Local styles are easy to use, but they aren't perfect. They tend to clutter up the HTML code, which was exactly what CSS was trying to avoid. Still, the technique is useful in a few circumstances, like this example.

Making use of ids and classes

CSS is pretty useful because it allows you to quickly add a style to all the elements of a particular type. For example, you can very easily make all the paragraphs on a page have the same color. But what if you want to apply a style to only a single element? And what if you have two kinds of paragraphs that should have different styles?

Figure 5-3 illustrates the CSS way to solve exactly these problems.

Figure 5-3

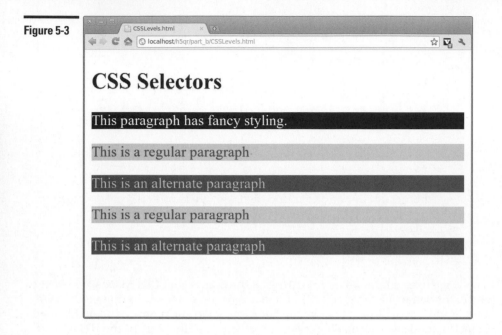

The CSSLevels.html page mainly consists of paragraphs, but there are three different paragraph styles. Ordinary paragraphs are light blue with dark blue letters. There are two special kinds of paragraphs. One paragraph has a special name (fancy). The fancy paragraph has its own styling. There is only one "fancy" paragraph, but there are two paragraphs using the "alternate" style. Take a look at the code and then I explain how it all works.

```
<!DOCTYPE HTML>
<html lang = "en">
<head>
  <title>CSSLevels.html</title>
  <meta charset = "UTF-8" />
  <style type = "text/css">
    p {
      background-color: lightblue;
      color: blue
    }

    #fancy {
      background-color: black;
      color: white;
    }

    .alternate {
```

```
      background-color: blue;
      color: lightblue;
    }

  </style>
</head>

<body>
  <h2>CSS Selectors</h2>
  <p id = "fancy">
    This paragraph has fancy styling.
  </p>

  <p>
    This is a regular paragraph.
  </p>

  <p class = "alternate">
    This is an alternate paragraph.
  </p>

  <p>
    This is a regular paragraph.
  </p>

  <p class = "alternate">
    This is an alternate paragraph.
  </p>

</body>
</html>
```

First, take a look at the HTML. It's almost the same, but I've added some special indicators to some of the paragraphs,

- **Ordinary paragraphs:** These paragraphs don't require any special features. They will be styled according to the regular p style rule.

- **Named paragraphs:** The first paragraph has an id property. This property allows you to specify a name for any HTML object. The id must be unique, meaning that only one object on the screen can have any particular id. The id can be anything you want, but it should be one word without spaces or punctuation. If an object has an ID, you can apply a style to that particular id.

- **Paragraphs in a class:** In addition to the id property, you can assign a class to any HTML element. The class attribute allows you to indicate that an element is a member of a particular class. Unlike the id, you can have as many elements in the same class as you want. The alternate paragraphs all have the `class` attribute set to `alternate`. You can use any term you want as a class name, but it should not have spaces or punctuation. You can apply a style to all elements with a certain class. Different kinds of elements can all have the same class, so you can apply the same class to paragraphs and headings if you want.

Once you've applied ids and classes in the HTML, you can modify the CSS code to apply styles to the various elements.

Use the number sign (#) in front of the id in your CSS to indicate you want to style an element with that id. For example, this code styles anything with the id `fancy`:

```
#fancy {
   background-color: black;
   color: white;
}
```

Use the period in front of a class name to define a style for a particular class. For example, you can style all elements of the `alternate` class with this code:

```
.alternate {
   background-color: blue;
   color: lightblue;
}
```

Use the id approach when you want to apply a style to an individual element in the page. Use the tag name when you want to attach a style to all the elements of a certain type. Use the class mechanism when you want to attach to a number of elements that may or may not be the same type.

Managing levels of CSS

CSS code can be added to a page in these three different ways:

- ✔ **Locally inside the HTML body:** You can apply a style directly to most HTML tags using the `style` attribute. This technique is illustrated in the "Employing local styles" section earlier in this part.

- ✔ **At the page level in the header:** This technique uses a `<style></style>` pair inside the head of the HTML page. This is a good way to specify styles for a specific page.

- ✔ **In an external document:** A style can be specified in a separate document and then referenced from a Web page. This approach allows you to share a set of style rules among several pages. It also cleans up the main page, as the styles are moved out of the way.

Figure 5-4 demonstrates a simple page that uses an external style sheet.

Figure 5-4

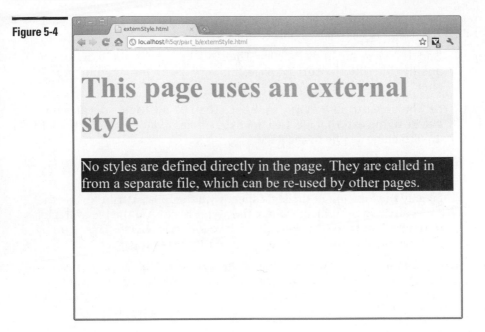

When you look at the source code for Figure 5-4, you'll see no CSS at all!

```
<!DOCTYPE HTML>
<html lang = "en">
<head>
  <title>externStyle.html</title>
  <meta charset = "UTF-8" />
  <link rel = "stylesheet"
        type = "text/css"
        href = "externStyle.css" />
</head>
<body>
  <h1>This page uses an external style</h1>

  <p>
    No styles are defined directly in the page.  They are
called in from
    a separate file, which can be reused by other pages.
  </p>
</body>
</html>
```

The interesting thing about this listing is how the page clearly has a style, but the style information is not directly present on the page. The secret is the link tag apparent in the header. This tag allows you to bring in a style from a separate page. To build an external link, follow these steps:

1. Add a <link> tag in the header. The link tag allows you to associate another file with the current page. It is very useful for attaching a style sheet to a Web page.

2. Set the rel attribute to stylesheet. The rel attribute specifies the nature of the external file. Use the stylesheet value to indicate that you are attaching a style to the page.

3. Set the type to text/css. Linked styles are indicated as text/css just like embedded styles (the ones created with the style tag).

4. Specify the location of the style sheet with the href attribute. Use the href attribute to indicate where the style sheet is on the file system. It's normally best to use a relative reference for style sheets. This allows you to move the page and the style sheet to the server together.

5. You can use the same style sheet over and over. Multiple pages can use the same style sheet. This is perfect if you have one site that will have many pages using the same style. You can then change the style on one page, and the new style will be reflected through the entire site.

The external style is another standard text file that can also be edited with a plain-text editor. It simply contains the style rules. It does not require the <style></style> pair. Here's the externStyle.css page called by externStyle.html:

```
h1 {
    color: red;
  background-color: yellow;
}

p {
  color: white;
  background-color: black;
}
```

Managing the Appearance of Your Page

Of course, Web pages do much more than change color. You can modify the main areas of a page by changing the appearance of text, adding borders and background images, and changing the overall layout.

Comprehending hex colors

For basic colors (like red and yellow) the color names are perfectly fine, but sometimes you need something with a little more sophistication. Color names are a bit confusing, and there are only sixteen color names guaranteed to be understood by CSS. It's also a bit difficult to adjust colors. For example, ask yourself what color has just a little more green than aqua?

CSS has a more specific way of indicating colors. It's a little geeky, but very powerful. Each dot on a computer monitor is actually three different tiny color emitters: red, green, and blue. The computer can adjust the amount of color that comes out of each of these emitters. If you want to see a red dot, the red emitter is turned to full strength and the green and blue emitters are turned completely off. You can combine the emitters to get various colors, so red and green makes blue.

 You might be confused that red and green makes blue, because in elementary school art class, they taught you a totally different way of mixing colors. Both are actually correct. In elementary school, you start with white paper and use pigments to subtract color values. Paper art normally works in a subtractive color model (as does your computer printer). The monitor starts with blackness and adds various amounts of colored light, so it evokes an *additive* color model. While the approach is different, the result is the same.

If you want to specify a particular color in the computer world, you can specify how much red, green, and blue (respectively) are used to make the color. It would make sense then for red to be the color 100, 0, 0. This would mean "turn on all the red, and turn off all the green and blue."

However, computers don't work as naturally with percentages as we do. Computer organization works in a different way, so color values actually range from 0 to 255. (Ack.) To make it even worse, technical people often convert these numbers to base 16 (hexadecimal notation), which brings in all kinds of crazy numbers and even letters. Each value (red, green, or blue) takes a two-digit value that ranges from 00 (completely off) to FF (full brightness). This funky system is called *hexadecimal* notation (often abbreviated *hex*).

Don't panic. It's not that hard. Look at the color tester program shown in Figure 5-5.

Feel free to look at the source code to see how it works. For now, use the program to see how these hex values can be used to specify colors.

First, note how the page is arranged.

- ✔ **The page background is black.** The page background will change colors to reflect the current color settings.

- ✔ **There are three columns of buttons.** There are columns for red, green, and blue.

- ✔ **Gray buttons directly set hex values.** The gray buttons can be used to set a color value to a specific setting. Brighter values (FF) are on the top of the stack, with lower values (00) on the bottom.

Figure 5-5

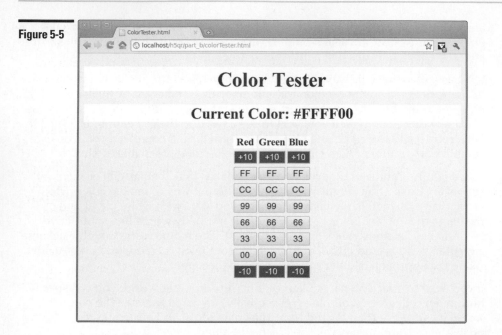

✔ **The current color is modified on the fly.** As you click the various buttons, the background color changes to reflect the current color, and the heading changes to indicate the hex value of the current color.

✔ **Gray buttons show preset values.** Web developers often begin with preset values in the ranges shown on the buttons (00, 33, 66, 99, CC, and FF). These values provide a reasonable range of colors while being easy to modify.

✔ **Black buttons allow finer tuning.** Of course, you can use values besides the presets. If you want to add a little more red, for example, you can use the +10 button in the red column to do this.

You can use hex color values anywhere you use color names. For example, if you want to specify that a heading level one is red text on a yellow background, you can use these hex codes:

```
h1 {
  color: #FF0000;
  background-color: #FFFF00;
}
```

Use the pound sign (#) to indicate that you are using hex values rather than color names. Hex values have a number of advantages over named colors.

✔ **There are more of them.** Only 16 named colors are officially recognized by CSS (although most browsers can read many more). With the hex system, you can actually represent more than 16 million different colors. Even if you stick with the 00336699CCFF system, you have 216 colors to play with.

✔ **Hex colors are easier to adjust.** You can directly tweak the hex values to get variations of the basic colors. If you want "a little more blue," this is much easier accomplished with hex colors than named colors.

✔ **Hex colors are more universal.** Most computer graphic programs use the hex notation, so you can sample a color in your graphics editor and match it in your Web page.

✔ **Color scheme generators can help you match colors.** If you have a design disability (like I do), you can use a tool like the color scheme generator at `http://colorschemedesigner.com`. This marvelous tool lets you play around with various color schemes in real time, and then generates the hex codes you can use in your own page.

TIP

HTML5 now sports some alternate ways of handling color, including the new HSB model and color with transparency. *See* Part 6 for more information on these new developments.

Editing text

Web pages are primarily about text, and CSS has many great features for manipulating text. Figure 5-6 shows a page with a number of text effects:

Figure 5-6

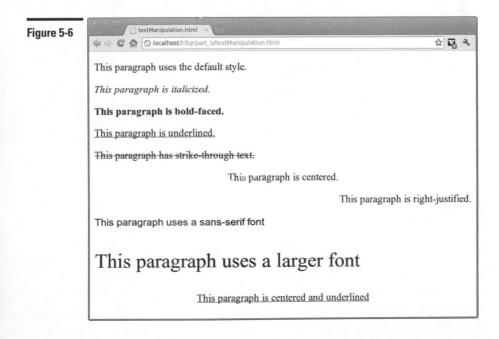

Text can be manipulated in a number of interesting ways. Look over the HTML source of the `textManipulation.html` page to see the general overview.

```html
<!DOCTYPE HTML>
<html lang = "en">
  <head>
    <title>textManipulation.html</title>
    <meta charset = "UTF-8" />
    <link rel = "stylesheet"
          type = "text/css"
          href = "textManipulation.css" />
  </head>

<body>

  <p>
    This paragraph uses the default style.
  </p>

  <p class = "italic">
    This paragraph is italicized.
  </p>

  <p class = "bold">
    This paragraph is bold-faced.
  </p>

  <p class = "underline">
    This paragraph is underlined.
  </p>

  <p class = "strikeThrough">
    This paragraph has strike-through text.
  </p>

  <p class = "center">
    This paragraph is centered.
  </p>

  <p class = "right">
    This paragraph is right-justified.
  </p>

  <p class = "sans">
    This paragraph uses a sans-serif font
  </p>
```

```
    <p class = "big">
      This paragraph uses a larger font.
    </p>

    <p class = "center underline">
      This paragraph is centered and underlined
    </p>
  </body>
</html>
```

There isn't too much going on here because most of the work happens in the CSS. Here are the things to notice:

- ✔ **The page is mainly a series of paragraphs.** There's no real styling in the HTML itself.

- ✔ **Styles are indicated by class identifiers.** Each paragraph has a class identifier to specify how it should be styled. You'll find a corresponding class definition in the style sheet.

- ✔ **The page calls an external style sheet.** The styles are handled by `text-Manipulation.css`.

- ✔ **One paragraph uses more than one style.** The last paragraph actually combines two classes. It calls both the `center` and `underline` classes.

The style sheet is where all the fun stuff happens. It uses a number of CSS rules to clarify how the various paragraphs should be styled. Look at the overall code, and then I break it down to show the details.

```
    .italic {
      font-style: italic;
    }

    .bold {
      font-weight: bold;
    }

    .underline {
      text-decoration: underline;
    }

    .strikeThrough {
      text-decoration: line-through;
    }

    .center {
      text-align: center;
```

```
    }

    .right {
      text-align: right;
    }

    .sans {
      font-family: sans-serif;
    }

    .big {
      font-size: 200%;
    }
```

You can see that I've defined a number of classes. The class names indicate the various effects, and each class contains a single rule to generate that effect.

Here's how all the various rules work:

✔ **Setting the font style:** You can set the overall font style with the `font-style` attribute. Valid options for this rule are `italic`, `normal`, and `oblique` (tipped backwards).

✔ **Changing text weight:** You can specify how much weight (boldness) to apply to text with the `font-weight` attribute. The most common values are `bold` and `normal`.

✔ **Managing text-decoration:** The `text-decoration` attribute can modify a number of effects, but it is normally used to add a line to text. The most commonly used values are `underline`, `overline`, `line-through`, and `none`.

✔ **Handling text alignment:** Text alignment is normally controlled through the (aptly named) `text-align` attribute. Most common values are `center`, `left`, `right`, and `justify`. Note that this attribute is used to align text inside an element only. If you want to center an entire element (say a paragraph or table), look ahead to the `margin` attributes described in the "Cleaning Up the Form" section later in this part.

✔ **Managing fonts:** You can specify a font to display with the `font-family` attribute. This can be used to specify any font on your system, but users will not be able to see these fonts if they aren't installed. Part 6 explains the wonderful new font techniques that overcome these problems.

✔ **Changing font size:** The size of your text can be specified with the `font-size` attribute. This attribute can be measured in many ways, but the safest approach for Web development is to specify percentage of the base font. To make text twice as large as normal, set its `font-size` to `200%`. (You can use traditional measures like points, but they have less meaning and reliability in the Web setting than in standard print application.)

Joining the border patrol

It's possible to draw a border around an element. This is a potentially useful design element, but it can also be very helpful when debugging a page layout. There are three main border properties:

- ✔ **border-width:** Specifies the width of the border. This can use the standard CSS measurement schemes, but borders are usually measured in pixels (px).

- ✔ **border-color:** Determines the color of the border. Border color is specified with a color name or hex value.

- ✔ **border-style:** Specifies a pattern for the border.

Figure 5-7 shows the possible border styles.

Figure 5-7

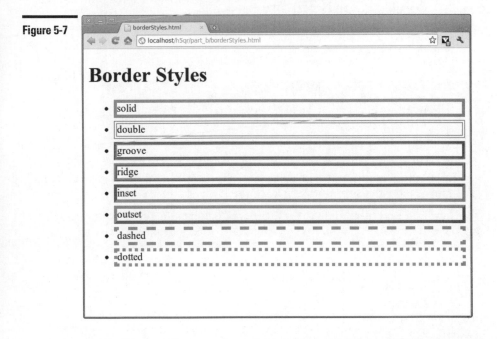

Generally, the various border attributes are combined into the single `border` property, which allows you to specify width, style, and color all in one. For example, to specify a 5-pixel blue double border on your paragraphs, you could use the following code:

```
p {
  border: 5px double blue;
}
```

One more handy trick is to isolate the various parts of the border to get lines. For example, you can specify `border-top` to draw a line above an element, and `border-right` to draw to the right of the element. Each of these miniborders can be given the same list of value as the standard border.

Putting in background images

You can add a background image to any element. The background attribute has a slightly different format from some of the other elements you've seen so far. Figure 5-8 illustrates a page with a background image.

Figure 5-8

Background images are added through CSS:

```
<!DOCTYPE HTML>
<html lang = "en">
  <head>
    <title>backgroundImage.html</title>
    <meta charset = "UTF-8" />
    <style type = "text/css">
      body {
        background-image: url("ropeBG.jpg");
      }
      h1 {
        background-image: url("ropeBGLight.jpg");
```

```
      }
      p {
        background-color: white;
      }
    </style>
  </head>

  <body>
    <h1>Using Background Images</h1>

    <p>
      The heading uses a lighter version of the background,
      and the paragraph uses a solid color background.
      The heading uses a lighter version of the background,
      and the paragraph uses a solid color background.
      The heading uses a lighter version of the background,
      and the paragraph uses a solid color background.
    </p>
  </body>
</html>
```

The key to adding background images is the `background-image` attribute. Here's how you use it:

1. Identify the image you want to use. Choose a background image carefully. Make sure the image supports the ideas you're trying to communicate and doesn't distract from your message. Any of the standard Web formats (`png`, `gif`, or `jpg`) are fine. You may want to adjust your image in an editor (IrfanView and Gimp are excellent free options) to ensure it's the right size and resolution.

2. Place the image in the same directory as your page. Although this step isn't absolutely necessary, it's much easier to manage images if they are physically close to your page. That way when you move the page to a server, you can easily move the associated images as well.

3. Build your page as normal. Create the XHTML code as you normally do.

4. Add a background image to the body tag. This will apply an image to the entire page. Of course, you can also apply images to any other element you want.

5. Specify the URL of your image. The value of the background image has a unique syntax. You must specify that you're invoking a URL, so if the image is `background.png`, the value of the `background-image` attribute will be `url("background.png")`.

6. Consider modifying the background. You can change the background image by using a number of other CSS attributes: `background-repeat`

allows you to control how the background repeats, and `background-position` lets you manipulate the position of the background.

7. Test your page. Make sure your background image is not too distracting.

Background images can be problematic. Take a look at Figure 5-9 for an example of this phenomenon:

Figure 5-9

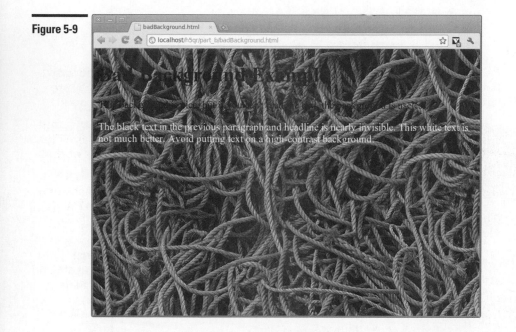

Inappropriate background images are one of the most common beginner mistakes. Consider the number of Web pages you've seen that have unreadable text.

Most interesting photos have a lot of contrast. This is great for a picture that's meant to grab the user's attention, but it's a problem when the image is supposed to be in the background. High contrast grabs the user's attention, which is a problem when the user is trying to read text. There are a couple of standard solutions to this problem. You can either provide lower-contrast versions of your background images, or you can use plain colors as the background of elements that feature text.

If you look back at Figure 5-9, you'll see that I use both of these tricks. The entire page has the rope background (thanks to Julian Burgess for the great image), but the title has a lighter version of the image — and the paragraphs use a solid color background.

You can create a lower-contrast version of an image using a tool like IrfanView. (Use the adjust colors tool to make an extremely dark or extremely light version of your image.) Use a darker background with lighter text, or a lighter background with darker text. Better yet, look to Part 6 for information on how to make partially transparent backgrounds with CSS. This allows you to add a high-contrast background that still allows you to see the underlying image.

Using Float Positioning

Page layout has long been one of the biggest weaknesses of HTML. Table-based hacks used to be the best way to get a page to act correctly, but now CSS provides a number of useful tools for managing the position of elements.

Thefloating-position works by defining the relationships between elements rather than specifying exactly where each element goes exactly. This can be a hard idea to get your head around, but once you understand how floating positions work, it is an extremely flexible and useful system.

Once you get the idea, you can use floating positions to set up a page that works very well on a variety of browsers. As an example, think of a standard HTML/ XHTML form. Figure 5-10 shows a typical form with no CSS applied.

Figure 5-10

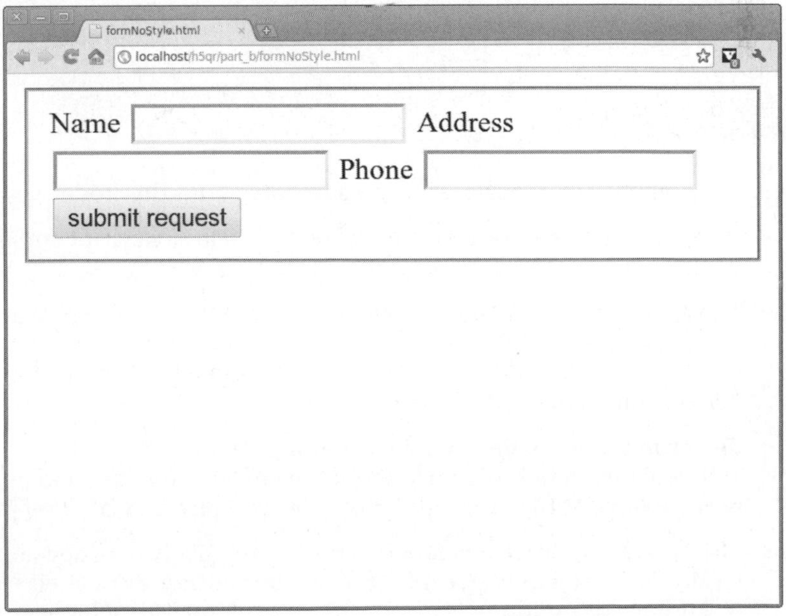

The form has all the necessary features, but it is ugly. Take a look at the HTML code to see how it is formatted:

```
<!DOCTYPE HTML>
<html lang = "en">
  <head>
    <title>formNoStyle.html</title>
    <meta charset = "UTF-8" />
  </head>

  <body>
    <form action = "">
      <fieldset>
        <label>Name</label>
        <input type = "text"
               id = "txtName" />
        <label>Address</label>
        <input type = "text"
               id = "txtAddress" />
        <label>Phone</label>
        <input type = "text"
               id = "txtPhone" />
        <button type = "button">
          submit request
        </button>
      </fieldset>
    </form>
  </body>
</html>
```

There are a number of important features to note about this code:

- ✔ **It supports a form.** Form elements are critical in JavaScript coding, and you'll be building a lot of forms in your travels.

- ✔ **The form has a `fieldset` container.** Most of the form elements are `inline` elements. (That is, they must exist inside a block element.) The `fieldset` tag is a special block element designed to live in a form, so it's a perfect container for form elements.

- ✔ **The form has a number of labels and inputs.** Most forms have this general structure: labels to indicate what the user is to enter, and input elements to accept the user input. Each row is typically a label/input pair.

- ✔ **The `label` tag describes labels.** This is a relatively new development in HTML. The `label` tag doesn't have any formatting associated with it, so it was not used traditionally. With CSS, you can provide whatever formatting you want.

✔ **The last element is a button.** Most forms include one or more buttons. The real action happens when the user clicks a button. Because the button will have different formatting than the input elements, I use the `button` tag to describe it.

✔ **No formatting is described in the HTML.** The HTML code simply describes the *intention* of the various elements, not their formatting. CSS will handle that.

✔ **The HTML is self-explanatory.** You can tell what everything is just by looking at the code. There's no code here that isn't directly related to the purpose of the form.

✔ **It's kind of like a table.** The general structure of the form looks a bit like a table, but not quite. The goal of the CSS is to take this very clean data structure and make it look *visually* like a table without having to muddy the HTML code with actual table tags.

When you look at Figure 5-10 it's clear that the browser is not displaying the form in a way that's acceptable. Typically, we want forms to look more like a table. Of course, you can embed an HTML table into the code, but that's a lot more work (and complexity) than you need. CSS provides a simpler solution.

Getting to know the display types

To understand how to make a form display like a table, you need to understand a little about how Web browsers manage page layout.

It takes very little CSS code to turn the form into a basic table-style format, but the code can be mysterious. The secret has to do with the way HTML lays out pages. Essentially, a Web browser can lay out Web elements in these three different ways:

✔ **Inline:** Place the element exactly where you would place the next character of text.

✔ **Block:** The element is basically independent and gets its own line. Block elements (like h1 tags and paragraphs) typically have line breaks before and after themselves.

✔ **Alternative:** Some special CSS attributes remove elements from the normal layout scheme (at least to some extent) and apply different placement rules to them. The `float` attribute described in this section is one example.

All the HTML tags have their own default display mechanism (inline or block). You can alter the way a tag is displayed by changing its `display` attribute. You can also add an alternative placement scheme by changing other CSS attributes. That's how you can make a form look and act like a table without needing table tags.

Having a block party

The first step in adjusting this form to act like a table is to define some of the elements as block-level using the `display` attribute.

Take a look at Figure 5-11 to see how this is done.

Figure 5-11

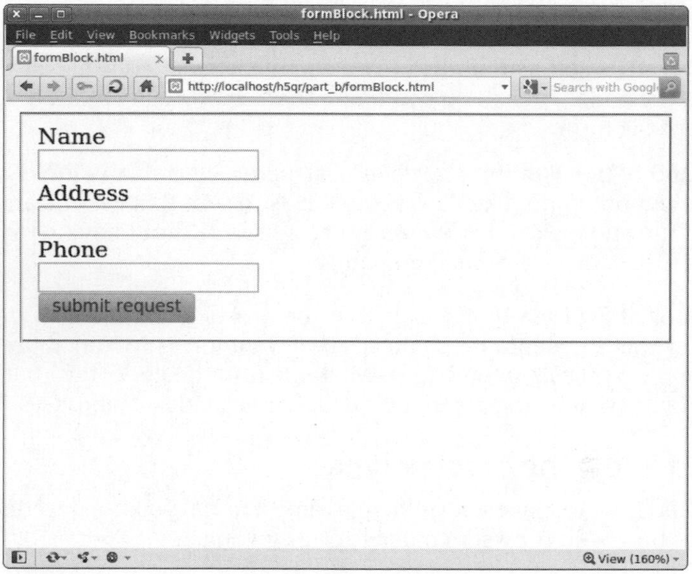

The HTML in `formBlock.html` is no different from the HTML in `formNoStyle.html`. The only difference is the inclusion of an external stylesheet: `formBlock.css`.

The code for `formBlock.css` is pretty simple:

```
input {
    display: block;
}

button {
    display: block;
}
```

All the code does is specify that buttons and input elements (the text boxes) should be block-level elements. This forces the page to a stacked look, but more importantly, it sets the stage for a nicer layout.

Note that I manually changed the text (using Ctrl-+) on all the screenshots in this chapter to make them easier to read in the book. The CSS doesn't change the size of the text, but of course, you could use it to do this if you want.

Floating to a two-column look

This is a starting place, but you really want the labels to be to the left of the corresponding block. The `float` attribute can be used to create exactly this effect, as you can see in Figure 5-12.

Figure 5-12

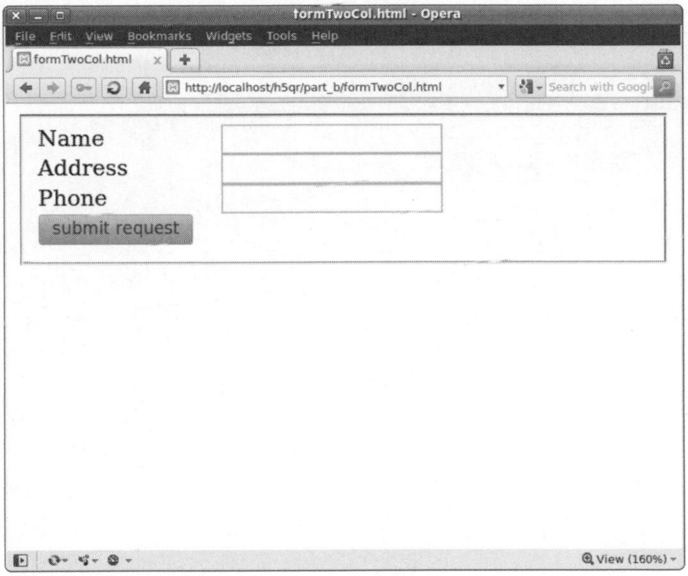

The `float` attribute allows you to remove an element from the normal layout rules and apply a special floating behavior. The `float` attribute describes the relationship between an element and its neighbors. In this case, I tell each label to float to the left. (You can also float to the right, but this is rarely done in practice.) This causes the label to be immediately to the left of the corresponding input element. Adding a width to the floated label makes the input elements line up nicely (looking and acting like a table with no additional HTML code).

Here's the code for `formTwoCol.css`:

```
label {
  float: left;
  width: 30%;
}

input {
  display: block;
}

button {
```

```
    display: block;
}
```

Cleaning up the form

Of course, there's a lot more you can do with the CSS to make things look better. `formFloat.html` in Figure 5-13 shows a nicely-formatted form.

Figure 5-13

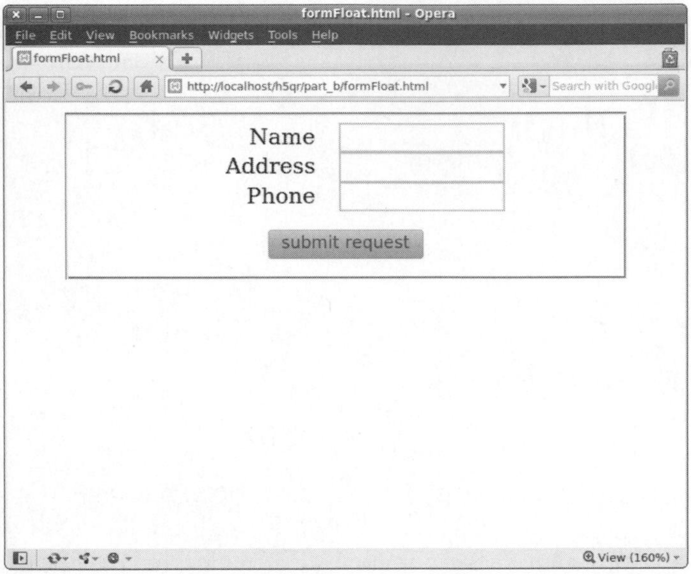

A few more CSS attributes are used to tweak the form's appearance:

- ✔ **margin:** Describes what margin occurs outside the boundary of an element. You can define all margins with the plain `margin` attribute, or you can specify individual margins. (`margin-left` controls the left margin, for example.) If you set the `margin` attribute to `auto`, you will center the element horizontally. (There is no easy way to do vertical centering in CSS.)

- ✔ **padding:** Specifies the space between the content of an element and its boundary. Padding is used to fix text that is crowded too close to a border.

- ✔ **text alignment:** Manipulates the content of an element (use the `margin` attribute to center the element itself).

Take a look at the code for `formFloat.css`, and then I explain how it works:

```
fieldset {
  width: 80%;
  margin: auto;
```

```
}

label {
   float: left;
   width: 30%;
   text-align: right;
   padding-right: 1em;
   margin-left: 15%;
}

input {
   display: block;
   width: 30%
}

button {
   display: block;
   margin: auto;
   margin-top: 1em;
}
```

This version of the CSS still works on exactly the same HTML as the previous examples. It adds a few formatting attributes to clean up the page and get a better-looking form. Here's how to build this type of form layout:

1. Begin with a two-column layout. Begin by building the simple two-column layout described in the previous section.

2. Center the fieldset. The fieldset is a block-level element by default, which is what you want. Block-level elements typically take up 100% of their container's width, so if you want to center a fieldset (or any other block-level element), you need to make it narrower and set the margin to auto.

3. Right-justify the labels. I think it's easier to enter data in a form if the label is very close to the text box. For that reason, I usually right-justify the labels. Set the labels' text-align attribute to right to achieve this effect.

4. Pad the labels a little bit. When text-align is set to right, the labels seem to crowd the input elements a bit. Add a little bit of padding-right to the labels to give them a little breathing space. (1em is the width of the widest character in the current font.)

5. "Center" the labels and input elements. You can't exactly center the label and input combination, as they're two different elements on the same line. However, you can use percentages to get the same effect. If the label and input are both set at 30% width and the left margin of the label is 20%, your label and input elements will be centered within the fieldset.

However, if you right-justify the labels (as I tend to do), the form looks better if you drift it a little more to the left. I actually set the `margin-left` of the label to 15% instead, because I think it looks better.

   6. Center the button. Although buttons can be created as HTML `input` elements, I tend to use the `<button>` tag instead. Buttons usually have different styles than input elements (because they don't require labels), so making them different HTML elements makes life easier. To center the button, just set its `display` attribute to `block` and the `margin` to `auto`. I find the button needs a little more vertical space, so I add a little `margin-top` to make it look a little better.

Of course, you can do much more to make your forms look better. You can add colors, background images, and custom fonts if you want. The important idea here is to let CSS handle all the formatting so your pages can look good with the cleanest possible HTML code. Separating the CSS from the HTML will make your life a lot easier when you start writing JavaScript code to manipulate the page.

Using absolute positioning

CSS allows some other useful mechanisms for positioning elements. The *absolute positioning* scheme is especially useful, as it allows you to have much more precise control of the position of CSS elements. When you specify that an element will use absolute positioning, you completely remove it from the normal inline/block calculations, and you are expected to specify the exact position of the object yourself.

This makes the absolute positioning scheme very powerful, but often too tedious for general layout. If you rely on absolute positioning to set up a page, you generally have to use the technique for every element on the screen. Absolute positioning techniques are best used for specialty objects that can ignore the rest of the page layout scheme. I use it mainly for creating moving objects that are animated with JavaScript.

Figure 5-14 shows an example of absolute positioning.

The bug shown in Figure 5-14 is sitting on top of the paragraph. This effect is possible with absolute positioning.

When you use *absolute positioning,* you manually specify the position of the element. Here's the HTML for the `absolute.html` demonstration:

```
<!DOCTYPE HTML>
<html lang = "en">
  <head>
    <title>absolute.html</title>
    <meta charset = "UTF-8" />
    <link rel = "stylesheet"
          type = "text/css"
```

```
                 href = "absolute.css" />
  </head>

  <body>
    <h1>Absolute Positioning Example</h1>
    <p>
      This page seems to have a bug in it!!!
      This page seems to have a bug in it!!!
      This page seems to have a bug in it!!!
      This page seems to have a bug in it!!!
      This page seems to have a bug in it!!!
      This page seems to have a bug in it!!!
      This page seems to have a bug in it!!!
      This page seems to have a bug in it!!!
    </p>

    <p id = "bug">
      <img src = "bug.gif"
           alt = "bug picture" />
    </p>

  </body>
</html>
```

Figure 5-14

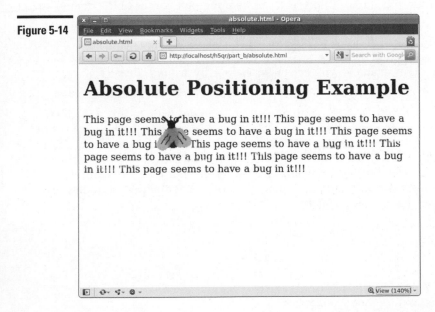

This page contains an ordinary paragraph and a second paragraph named "bug". The bug paragraph contains only an image of a bug. Note that images are inline-level tags, and they must be embedded within a block-level tag to make the page validate. That's why the image is inside another element, and it's the paragraph element that will be manipulated.

If there were no CSS, the page would simply display the bug image as its own separate paragraph after the ordinary (text-laden) paragraph. However, the CSS file changes things:

```
#bug {
  position: absolute;
  left: 100px;
  top: 50px;
}
```

The CSS changes the behavior of the element named bug in a few important ways:

✔ **The position attribute is set to absolute.** This means that the ordinary layout mechanisms will be overruled by specific position information.

✔ **The left attribute is set to 100 px (pixels).** Once you've assigned absolute positioning to an element, you're committed to specifying its top and left positions. Normally absolutely positioned elements are set using pixels (px).

✔ **The top attribute is set to 50 px.** This forces the object's upper-left corner to be (100, 50) pixels from the upper-left corner of the document.

✔ **The element will obscure traditional elements.** Anything placed with absolute positioning will ignore previously positioned elements. This can be a problem in ordinary Web design, but in animation, it can be a nice feature. (For example, you can make the bug fly around the screen with JavaScript tricks.)

There is much more to CSS positioning than I can describe in this introductory part. If you want to investigate CSS positioning in more detail, please check out one of my other books: *HTML, XHTML, and CSS All-in-One For Dummies, 2nd edition* (Wiley). I have hundreds of pages in that book dedicated to explaining multicolumn layouts, drop-down menus, and other CSS goodness. Of course, you can also check Part 6 for some wonderful new CSS capabilities, including an entirely new layout mechanism.

New and Improved CSS Elements

In addition to changes in HTML, there have been some striking new changes in Cascading Style Sheets (CSS) technology. Now almost all of the page formatting, style, and layout is performed by CSS. This part describes those features of CSS3 that are relatively new, are supported (or are expected to be supported), and have a potential significant impact on the Web. As you work with these CSS elements, you'll notice that many of them are not fully implemented. The major rendering engines have created vendor-specific test versions of many of these tags:

- **-webkit-:** This indicates a test version of the attribute optimized for browsers based on the WebKit rendering engine. This includes Safari, Chrome, and the iPhone browsers.

- **-o-:** This prefix stands for the Opera browser. It's not used very often because Opera tends to either support an attribute completely or not at all. The Opera rendering engine is (naturally enough) used in the Opera browser. You'll also see versions of the Opera browser on many portable devices.

- **-moz-:** The -moz- prefix is used for test versions of an attribute optimized for the Mozilla rendering engine. This is primarily Firefox, but a number of other Mozilla-based browsers are starting to appear.

IE8 supports almost none of the features described in this part. IE9 promises fuller support for HTML5 standards (and hopefully support for CSS3).

As always, be sure to check out my Web site for working examples of every code fragment in the book: www.aharrisbooks.net/h5qr.

In this part . . .

- **Introducing New CSS3 Selection Tools**
- **Taking a Look at Font and Text Support**
- **Examining the Flexible Box Layout Model**
- **Previewing New Visual Elements**

CSS3's New Selection Tools

One key element of CSS is the way a developer can select parts of the page for markup. Traditional CSS has allowed selection by tag type (p to select all paragraphs, for example), by class (.fancy indicates a style applied to all elements with the fancy class), or by id (#sidebar indicates a style that will be applied to an element with the sidebar id).

CSS3 supports several new selectors with interesting new capabilities.

Attribute selection

You can now apply a style to any element with a specific attribute value. For example, the input tag takes many different forms, all determined by the type attribute. If you apply a single style to the input element, that style is applied to many different kinds of elements: check boxes, text fields, and radio buttons. By using the new attribute syntax, you can apply a style to any particular type of input element:

```
input[type="text"]{
   background-color: #CCCCFF;
}
```

You can apply the style with or without a tag type, but it's possible to have unexpected side effects if you choose an extremely common attribute.

not

There are times you want an inverse selection. For example, imagine you wanted to apply a style to all the paragraphs that are not members of the special class:

```
p:not(.special) {
   border: 1px solid red;
}
```

The given code will apply the solid red border to any paragraph that does not have the special class assigned.

nth-child

The nth-child selector allows you to select one or more elements in a group. The basic version uses a numeric input:

```
#myList>li:nth-child(1){
   border: 1px solid blue;
}
```

This allows you to apply a style to the first of a group of elements. In my example, I have a list with four items. The style is applied to the list items, not the list.

(It seems to me that the list items are children of the list, so it should be the nth-child of the list — but nobody asked me.)

The numeric value can actually be a formula, like an+b. If you love algebra (and who doesn't?), you can select all the even-numbered elements like this:

```
#myList>li:nth-child(2n){
   border: 1px solid blue;
}
```

A similar formula can be used to pick the odd-numbered children:

```
#myList>li:nth-child(2n+1){
   border: 1px solid blue;
}
```

You could use this formula system to get all kinds of groupings (every third element with 3n, for example), but most people simply need a particular element, or all the even or odd rows. CSS3 supplies shortcut keywords — even and odd — so you don't have to do it using math:

```
#myList>li:nth-child(even){
   color: white;
   background-color: red;
}
```

The last keyword allows you to pick the last element from a group. There are a few more variations of this selection technique:

- ✔ **:nth-last-child(N):** Works just like nth-child, except it counts from the end of the group of elements rather than the beginning.

- ✔ **:nth-of-type(N):** This selector works just like nth-child, except it filters to a specific type and ignores any elements that are not of exactly the same type of element.

- ✔ **last-child:** This (naturally enough) selects the last child element.

- ✔ **last-nth-of-type(N):** Works like nth-of-type, but from the end of the group.

- ✔ **first-child:** Grabs the first element. (Technically, this was available in CSS2, but it was rarely used.)

 These selection tools are fully supported in all the recent browsers except IE. IE9 supports these tools, but older versions do not. However, as they are generally used simply to improve readability, it should be safe to use them. Non-compliant browsers will simply skip the style.

Other new pseudo-classes

Pseudo-classes allow you to specify styles based on the state of an element. Modern CSS supports a number of new pseudo-classes:

✔ **:hover:** The :hover pseudo-class has been a part of CSS from the beginning, but it was officially defined only for the <a> tag. Now the :hover pseudo-class can be applied to any element. If the mouse (or other pointing device) is over an element, that element has the hover state activated.

TIP

Note that mobile devices don't always support hover, because the position of the pointing device (the stylus or finger) isn't known until the item is activated. Mobile devices may have some sort of tabbing mechanism to indicate which item is being "hovered" over.

✔ **:focus:** This pseudo-class is activated when an element is ready to receive keyboard input.

✔ **:active:** A form element is active when it's currently being used. For example, when a button has been pressed but not yet released.

TIP

Mobile devices often skip directly to active mode without going through hover mode. This can be an important design consideration when using state for styling.

The state pseudo-classes are fully supported by all modern browsers except the IE family of browsers. There is limited (but buggy support) in early versions of IE.

Downloadable Fonts and Text Support

Font support has always been one of the biggest weaknesses of the HTML/CSS model. Although a Web developer can suggest any font for a Web page, the font files are traditionally a client-level asset — if the client doesn't have the font installed, she won't see it. Developers had to rely on a series of substitute fonts and fallbacks. Finally, CSS3 now supports a sensible solution for providing downloadable fonts.

@font-face

The @font-face style does not work like most CSS elements. It doesn't apply markup to some part of the page. Instead, it defines a new CSS value that can be used in other markup. Specifically, it allows you to place a font file on your server and define a font family using that font.

```
@font-face {
  font-family: "Miama";
  src: url("Miama.otf");
}
```

The `font-family` attribute indicates the name you will be giving this font in the rest of your CSS code. Typically, it's similar to the font filename, but this isn't required. The `src` attribute is the URL of the actual font file as it is found on the server. Once a font face has been defined, it can be used in an ordinary `font-family` attribute in the rest of your CSS code:

```
h1 {
    font-family: Miama;
}
```

While all modern browsers support the `@font-face` feature, the actual file types supported vary from browser to browser. Here are the primary font types:

- ✔ **TTF:** The standard TrueType format (TTF) is well-supported, but not by all browsers. Many open source fonts are available in this format.

- ✔ **OTF:** Similar to TTF, but it's a truly open standard and, as a result, is preferred by those who are interested in open standards. OTF (OpenType) is supported by most browsers except IE.

- ✔ **WOFF:** A proposed standard format currently supported by Firefox. Microsoft has hinted at supporting WOFF (Web Open Font Format) in IE9.

- ✔ **EOT:** Microsoft's proprietary embedded font format. EOT (Embedded OpenType) works only in IE, but to be fair, Microsoft has had embedded font support for many years.

You can use a font conversion tool like the free Online Font Converter (`http://onlinefontconverter.com`) to convert to whatever font format you prefer.

It's possible to supply multiple `src` attributes. This way, you can include both an EOT and OTF version of a font so that it will work on a wide variety of browsers.

Just because you can include a font doesn't mean you should. Think carefully about readability. Also, be respectful of intellectual property. There are many excellent free open source fonts available. Begin by looking at `http://openfontlibrary.org`.

Column support

Web developers have been looking for column support since the early days of HTML. Many approaches have been used over the years, including frames, tables, and floating elements. Finally, CSS3 has now integrated column support.

```
#main{
    column-count: 3;
    column-gap: 2em;
    column-rule: 5px double red;

    -webkit-column-count: 3;
```

```
        -webkit-column-gap: 2em;
        -webkit-column-rule: 5px double red;

        -moz-column-count: 3;
        -moz-column-gap: 2em;
        -moz-column-rule: 5px double red;

    } // end main
```

Three new rules govern columns:

- ✔ **column-count:** Indicates the number of columns.

- ✔ **column-gap:** The space between columns using standard CSS measurements.

- ✔ **column-rule:** The vertical line (if any) between the columns. This rule is defined with exactly the same parameters as the `border` rule.

Promising as the column system looks, it has a few problems:

- ✔ **It isn't supported.** The standard column rules are not yet supported by any major browsers. However, two of the main engines have their own variations of the column tags. Incorporate the `-moz-` versions of the tag for Firefox and related browsers. The `-webkit-` versions support Safari and Chrome.

- ✔ **Column width is automatic.** You can either set all columns to the same width (in which case the number of columns is automatically determined) or you can set the number of columns (which automatically determines a width for each). You cannot make one column a different size from the others.

- ✔ **Text flow is automatic.** Content fills up the entire area, automatically flowing from one column to the next. There is no easy way to specify which text is in which column.

It's tempting to consider use of the column CSS attributes as a page layout technique, but this doesn't seem to be a practical consideration yet. Also, since there is no support for columns in IE or Opera, it's still necessary to consider other more universal page layout techniques. (For one interesting new option, *see* "Flexible Box Layout Model" later in this part.)

Columns are more suited for magazine-style layout with text flowing among columns.

text-stroke

You can change the appearance of your fonts in another new way. With CSS3, you can specify a stroke color for your text. This defines an outline around the letter. You can specify the stroke color (using any of the standard CSS color values) as well as a stroke width (using the normal size attributes).

```
h2 {
  color: yellow;
  -webkit-text-stroke: 2px red;
  font-size: 300%;
}
```

Currently, no browsers support the `text-stroke` attribute directly, but WebKit-based browsers (Chrome and Safari) support the vendor-specific `-webkit-` version.

text-shadow

Shadows are another common feature of modern Web designs. Shadows add an element of depth to a page, but they can also enhance readability (if used properly) to lift a headline from the page. The `text-shadow` attribute was technically part of CSS2, but it has only recently been supported by major browsers:

```
h2 {
  font-size: 300%;
  text-shadow: 3px 3px 5px #666666;
}
```

The `text-shadow` attribute has four parameters:

- **offset-x:** Determines how far in the x-axis (left-right) the shadow will be from the original text. A positive value moves the shadow to the right, and a negative value moves to the left.

- **offset-y:** Indicates how far in the y-axis (up-down) the shadow will be from the original text. A positive value moves the shadow down, and a negative value moves the shadow up

- **blur:** Specifies the blur radius of the shadow. If the value is `0px`, there is no blur, and the shadow looks just like the original text. Generally, you'll want the blur equivalent to the longest of your offsets. This allows the shadow to be recognizable as a shadow of the text without becoming a distraction.

- **color:** Defines the shadow color. Generally, a dark gray is the standard shadow color, but you can also try other colors for special effects. Note that blurring tends to lighten the shadow color. If there's a great deal of blur applied, the shadow color can be the same color as the text. If the shadow will not be blurred much, you may need to lighten the shadow color for readability.

The size of the shadow is determined indirectly with a combination of offsets and blurs. You may have to experiment to get the shadow you're looking for.

A special case of text shadowing can be used to help text stand out against a background image. Apply a small shadow of a contrasting color.

All late-model browsers except IE support the `text-shadow` feature. No special prefixes are necessary.

Flexible Box Layout Model

Page layout has been a constant concern in Web development. There have been many different approaches to page layout, and all have weaknesses. The current standard is the floating mechanism. While this works quite well, it has two major weaknesses:

- **It can be hard to understand.** The various parts of the float specification can be difficult to follow, and the behavior is not intuitive. The relationship between `width`, `clear`, and `float` attributes can be difficult to follow.

- **The page order matters.** One goal of semantic layout is to completely divorce the way the page is created from how it is displayed. With the floating layout, the order in which various elements are written in the HTML document influences how they are placed. An ideal layout solution would allow any kind of placement through CSS, even after the HTML is finished.

While the floating mechanism is the current standard for page layout, clearly another option would be nice. CSS3 includes the new flexible box layout as an alternative.

Creating a flexible box layout

CSS3 proposes a new layout mechanism, flexible box. While it is far from complete, this mechanism shows significant promise. Here's essentially how it works. (I'm deliberately leaving out details here for clarity; *see* "Viewing a flexible box layout" later in this part.)

1. Designate a page segment as a box. The `display` attribute of most elements can be set to various types. CSS3 introduces a new display type: `box`. Setting the display of an element to `box` makes it capable of holding other elements with the flexible box mechanism.

2. Determine the orientation of child elements. Use a new attribute called `box-orient` to determine if the child elements of the current element will be placed vertically or horizontally inside the main element.

3. Specify the weight of child elements. Each child element can be given a numeric weight. The weight determines how much space that element takes up. If the weight is zero, the element takes as little space as possible. If the weight of all the elements is one, they all take up the same amount of space. If one element has a weight of two and the others all have a weight of one, the larger element has twice the size of the others, and so on. Weight is determined through the `box-flex` attribute.

4. Nest another box inside the first. You can nest flex boxes inside each other. Simply apply the `box` display type to inner elements, which will show the display.

5. Modify the order in which elements appear. Normally, elements will appear in the order in which they were placed on the page, but you can use the `box-ordinal-group` attribute to adjust the placement order.

Viewing a flexible box layout

As an example of the new layout mechanism (*see* "Creating a flexible box layout" earlier in this part), take a look at the following HTML code:

```
<div id = "a">
  <div id = "b">b</div>
  <div id = "c">c</div>
  <div id = "d">
    <div id = "e">e</div>
    <div id = „f">f</div>
  </div>
</div>
```

While this is a clearly made-up example, it shows a complex structure that could be difficult to style using standard layout techniques. Figure 6-1 illustrates a complex nested style that would be difficult to achieve through traditional layout techniques (for example, CSS2).

Figure 6-1

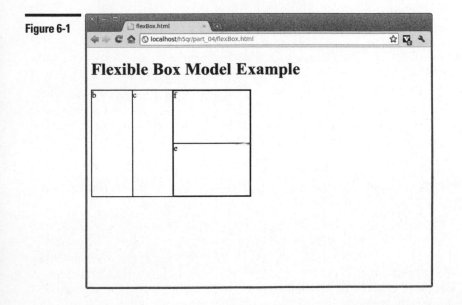

The following example style sheet is used to apply a floating style to this page:

```
div {
  border: 1px solid black;
}

#a {
  width: 300px;
  height: 200px;

  box-orient: horizontal;
  display: box;

 }

#b {
  box-flex: 1;
}

#c {
  box-flex: 1;
}

#d {
  display: box;
  box-orient: vertical;
  box-flex: 2;
}

#e {
  box-flex: 1;
  box-ordinal-group: 2;
}

#f {
  box-flex: 1;
}
```

The CSS looks complex, but there are only four new CSS elements. Here's how this specific example works:

1. Set up a to be the primary container. The a div is the primary container, so give it a height and width. It will contain flex boxes, so set the display attribute to box. Determine how you want the children of this box to be lined up by setting the box-orient attribute to vertical or horizontal.

2. Specify the weights of b, c, and d. In my example style sheet here, I want elements b and c to take up half the space, and d to fill up the remainder of the space. To get this behavior, set the `box-flex` value of c and d to 1, and the `box-flex` value of d to 2.

3. **Set up d as another container.** The d element will contain e and f. Use `display: box` to make d a flex container, and set `box-orient` to vertical to make the elements line up vertically. (Normally, nested elements will switch between horizontal and vertical.)

4. Elements e and f should each take half of d. Use the `box-flex` attribute to give these elements equal weight.

5. Change the ordinal group of e so it appears after f. The `box-ordinal-group` attribute indicates the order in which an element will be displayed inside its group. Normally, all items have a default value of 1, so they appear in the order they are written. You can demote an element by setting its `box-ordinal-group` value to a higher number, causing that element to be displayed later than normal. I set e to ordinal group 2, so it is displayed after element f.

. . . And now for a little reality

The flex box system seems perfect. It's much more sensible than the Byzantine layout techniques that are currently in use. However, the flexible box system is not ready for common use yet. Right now, not a single browser implements the flex box attributes directly. However, there are special vendor-specific versions available. WebKit-based browsers (primarily Safari and Chrome) use variations that begin with `-webkit-`, and Gecko-based browsers (Firefox and Mozilla) use the `-moz-` extension. To make the example in this part work in modern browsers, you need to include both `-webkit-` and `-moz-` versions of all the attributes, like this:

```
#a {
  width: 300px;
  height: 200px;

  -moz-box-orient: horizontal;
  display: -moz-box;

  -webkit-box-orient: horizontal;
  display: -webkit-box;
}

#b {
  -moz-box-flex: 1;
  -webkit-box-flex: 1;
}
```

At the moment, no version of IE supports the flex box model, but preliminary versions of IE9 do support the model. Surprisingly, Opera does not yet support this mechanism. Regardless, it looks like this could become an important layout technique, particularly on mobile devices that already include compliant browsers.

Some browsers have problems with multiple levels of nesting, but this is expected to be resolved. This technique is worth learning about, as it may well become the preferred layout technique in the future. See the file `flexTwoCol. html` on my Web site (`www.aharrisbooks.net/h5qr`) for an example of a standard two-column page using the flex box technique.

New Visual Elements

A large number of visual enhancements are available in upcoming versions of CSS. While none of them are essential, they add tremendous new options for developers.

Color values

CSS3 includes new ways of thinking about colors.

CSS3 also supports a new form of color representation that also incorporates transparency. You can now define a color in the RGBA format:

```
h1 {
  color: rgba(0, 0, 0, .3);
}
```

This format uses four numeric values. The first three are for red (r), green (g), and blue (b), respectively. Use standard 0–255 values to indicate the color you want. The fourth value (a) stands for *alpha,* which is another term for transparency. The alpha value is a real number between 0 (completely transparent) and 1 (completely opaque).

CSS3 also supports the flexible HSL color model. HSL stands for hue, saturation, and lightness. While the RGB model reflects the way colors are represented on the computer monitor, the HSL model is closer to the way most artists and designers actually work with colors. An HSL color requires three parameters:

✔ **hue:** An angle around the color wheel. Red is value 0 and 360, and the visible spectrum is wrapped around a circle. Use a value between 0 and 360 for hue. See the tool at `http://colorschemedesigner.com` for an example of a color wheel.

✔ **saturation:** Refers to the distance from gray, black, or white. A color with 0% saturation is gray, black, or white (depending on the lightness). A color with 100% saturation is the brightest form of the hue color. Saturation values are integers between 0 and 100 followed by a percent sign.

✔ **lightness:** Makes the color lighter or darker than the base color. Any color with 0% lightness will be black, and any color with 100% lightness will be white. Lightness values are integers between 0 and 100 followed by a percent sign.

You can assign an HSL color anywhere you can use colors:

```
background: hsl(0, 0%, 50%);
```

Colors can't be appreciated in a black-and-white book. Look at `hsl.html` on the Web site for this book (`www.aharrisbooks.net/h5qr/hsl.html`). It is an interactive example of the HSL color model. Change the values of hue, saturation, and lightness, and see a color sample change colors on the fly.

The HSL model is not exactly the same as the HSV model (hue, saturation, and value) often used in graphics programs (although they are similar). Both models use hue and saturation in essentially the same way. The `value` in HSV ranges from black to full saturation, where `lightness` in HSL ranges from black to white. Also, note that the term *luminance* is often used in color theory, but the L in HSL is not about luminance (which is a technical measurement of light energy) but about lightness.

CSS3 includes one more color model, HSLA. As you might guess, it is the HSL model with an alpha channel. The alpha channel indicates the level of transparency; an alpha channel with a value of 0 is fully transparent, and 1 is fully opaque.

```
background: hsla(0, 0%, 50%, 0.7);
```

Gradients

A *gradient* is a sequence of colors. Simple gradients flow from a foreground to a background color, but gradients can contain many other colors. There are also multiple types of gradients. The most common are *linear* (which flows in a straight line from one color to another) or *radial* (where one color is concentrated at a specific point, and the other colors are visible farther from that point).

Gradients have been used for some time in Web development as a nice way to add color. The primary way to handle gradients has been to build a thin gradient strip in an image editor and apply that image to the `background-image` attribute of an element.

Figure 6-2 illustrates the gradients described in this section.

Figure 6-2

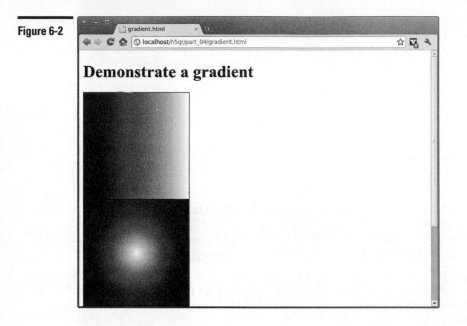

CSS3 suggests a structure to build gradients directly in the browser. These generated gradients can be used anywhere an image can be used (commonly as a background image).

Unfortunately, a standard syntax for the gradient has not yet been determined. The Mozilla and WebKit engines have differing approaches to the attribute. The Mozilla version is a bit easier to follow:

```
background-image:
    -moz-linear-gradient(left, blue, white);
```

Here's how you attach a Mozilla-style gradient to the background of an element:

1. Begin with an image attribute. The gradient isn't a stand-alone attribute. It is meant to be a replacement for an image. Use the `gradient` attribute wherever you would use an image.

2. Use the `-moz-linear-gradient` attribute. Mozilla uses different attributes for linear and radial gradients.

3. Specify the direction of the gradient. This gradient will go from left to right, so I specify `left`. (You can also specify a pixel value or percentage, but the special 'left' keyword is easy to remember.)

4. Indicate starting and ending colors. My gradient starts as blue and ends as white.

The WebKit-based browsers (Chrome, Safari, and iPhone) use a completely different syntax:

```
background-image:
  -webkit-gradient(
    linear,
    left center, right center,
    from(blue),
    to(white)
  );
```

The parameters are familiar, but slightly different from the Mozilla variant.

1. Attach the gradient to an image. The gradient does not stand on its own, but must be used where you would use an image.

2. Specify the gradient type. WebKit uses a single attribute for both gradient types. The first parameter indicates which type of gradient (linear in this example) will be created.

3. Indicate the beginning and ending position of the gradient. You can indicate how the gradient will flow. The value `left center, right center` tells the gradient to move from left to right; a `left top, right bottom` value would create a diagonal gradient, and so on.

4. Specify starting and ending colors. The `from()` and `to()` parameters are an easy way to create a two-color gradient. Each parameter accepts a color value. The gradient will always begin at the `from` value and end at the `to` value.

5. Add color-stops if you want. Between the `from` and `to` color, you can add as many `color-stop` elements as you want. Each `color-stop` takes two parameters: a percentage (0–1) and a color. The indicated color will appear at the percentage of the gradient indicated by the percentage.

Radial gradients are very similar to the linear variety. Again, the WebKit and Mozilla engines have different syntax. Here's the Mozilla-style radial gradient:

```
background-image:
  -moz-radial-gradient(white, blue);
```

It's a pretty simple syntax. Simply list the colors you want to display from inside to outside.

The WebKit version is more complex:

```
background-image:
  -webkit-gradient(
    radial,
```

```
         center center, 0,
         center center, 100,
         from(white),
         to(blue)
    );
```

In the WebKit model, linear and radial gradients use the same attribute with different parameters:

1. Make the gradient an image. As usual, the gradient does not appear on its own, but is part of an image element, usually `background-image`.

2. Set the gradient type to radial. The first parameter of the `-webkit-gradient` attribute is the type.

3. Determine the center and radius of the first color. Generally, the first color will be a point in the center. The value `center center, 0` indicates a value at the center of the element with a radius of zero.

4. Determine the center and radius of the second color. The second color will be the outer color. It will also generally be centered on the center of the element, but it will usually have a larger radius.

5. Specify starting and ending colors. Describe which colors will be displayed.

It is not clear which version will become the standard. (If you're a member of the W3C and you're asking me, I vote for the Mozilla model.)

Image borders

CSS 3 allows you to use an image for an element border. The mechanism is quite powerful, as it detects the edges of an image and slices it to create the edges and corners of the border from the edges and corners of the image.

For example, look at the simple picture frame image in Figure 6-3.

The frame image is stored as `frame.png` in the same directory as the HTML file. It has a transparent center. Apply the following code to add an image border around all `h2` elements on the page:

```
h2 {
   border-width: 15px;
   border-image: url("frame.png") 25% repeat;
   -webkit-border-image: url("frame.png") 25% repeat;
   -moz-border-image: url("frame.png") 25% repeat;
}
```

Figure 6-3

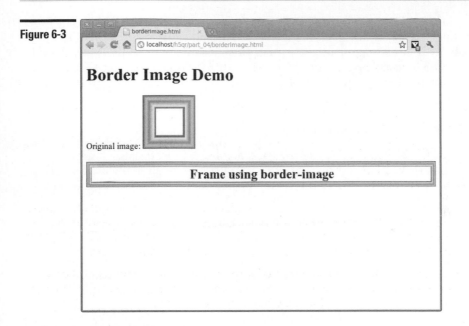

Here's how you add a border image:

1. Acquire your image. The image should already be designed as some sort of border. Typically, it will be a shape around the edges, with either a solid-color center or a transparent center. I usually make the image 100 × 100 pixels, so the math is easier to figure later.

2. Specify the border width. You'll need to indicate the border width directly. The border of the frame image will be scaled to fit whatever size you want.

3. Calculate how much of the image's border you want. I want to use the outer 25% of my frame image as the border, so I specify 25%. If you leave off the percent sign, the value will calculate in pixels. You can add four values if you prefer to use different amounts of the original image for each boundary.

4. Indicate the behavior you want. The original image will almost never be the same size as the element you're wanting to surround, so you can supply a tip to explain how the browser should handle elements larger than the original. The most common choices are `repeat` (repeat the original image) or `stretch` (stretch the image to take up the entire space). With a simple image like `frame.png` used in this example, the results will be the same.

Reflections

Reflection is another one of those visual elements that adds quite a bit to a page when done well. CSS3 promises to handle reflections using only CSS. Currently, only the WebKit-based browsers (that is, Safari, Mobile Safari, and Chrome) support this capability. However, it shows such promise that some form of this capability is likely to appear in the other browsers at some point. Apply the following CSS to make any element with the `reflect` class have a nice-looking reflection in the supported browsers:

```
-webkit-box-reflect: below 2px;
```

Basic reflections are quite simple:

1. Apply the `-webkit-box-reflect` attribute. Unfortunately, there is no generic version, nor has the `reflect` attribute been duplicated by other browsers.

2. Specify where the reflection is to be placed. Normally, the reflection goes beneath (`below`) the primary element, but it can also be `above`, `left`, or `right`.

3. Indicate a gap width. The reflection can be placed right next to the original element, but often it looks better with a small gap. The gap is normally measured in pixels.

This will produce a very nice reflection.

However, reflections aren't usually pixel-perfect duplications. They tend to fade out over distance. WebKit allows you to add a gradient to a reflection. In this case, the gradient will go from completely opaque (`white`) to completely transparent (`transparent`.) The `webkit` gradient model is a bit complex. (*See* "Gradients" earlier in this part for more details.) You can usually just use a variation of the gradient I supply in this example:

```
.reflect {
    -webkit-box-reflect: below 2px
      -webkit-gradient(
        linear,
        center top, center bottom,
        from(transparent),
        color-stop(.6, transparent),
        to(white));
}
```

The standard part of the reflection is just like the previous example, but it includes a gradient that will fade the reflection to transparency.

1. Build a linear gradient. The gradient for a reflection will nearly always be linear.

2. Make the gradient move from top to bottom. Use "`center top`" to indicate the top, and "`center bottom`" to indicate the bottom. These values

represent the top and bottom of the *original* image, not the reflection (which will, of course, be reversed.)

3. Begin with complete transparency. The top of the original image will be the bottom of the reflection, so begin with transparency. (Set `transparent` as the `from` color.)

4. Finish at complete opacity. This gradient isn't really about color, but about which parts of the reflection are visible. The bottom of the original image (which will be the top of the reflection) will be completely opaque. Set the `to` color to `white` to indicate opacity.

5. Add a color-stop to adjust the fade. The `color-stop` parameter allows you to add a new color. Add a color-stop to indicate where in the reflection you want the image to begin appearing. I set a second transparent color at 60%, so only the bottom 40% (or so) of the original image appears as the reflection.

Note that the reflected image is not calculated as a separate element for page layout purposes, so text and other content will flow right on top of your reflection.

Figure 6-4 shows a reflected image.

Reflections are commonly applied to images, but they can be applied to any element, even video!

Figure 6-4

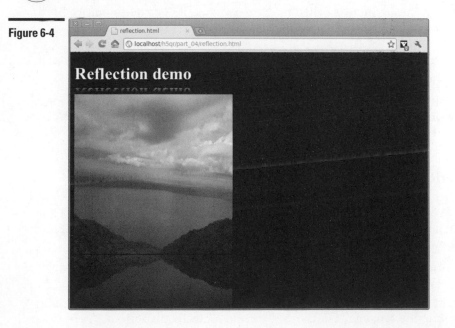

Rounded corners

Rounded corners have become a symbol of Web 3.0 design. It was quite difficult to create cross-platform round corners in previous versions of CSS, but CSS3 makes this quite easy.

The following CSS makes a nice-looking blue heading:

```
h1 {
  width: 60%;
  background-color: #000066;
  color: #9999ff;
  border: #9999ff 3px groove;
  margin: auto;
  text-align: center;
  border-radius: 10px;
}
```

Almost all of the code is garden-variety CSS2. The one new element is the `border-radius` attribute. This attribute allows you to specify a rounding parameter for the corners. Each corner will be replaced by a small arc. The rounding parameter determines the radius of that arc. A value of `1em` will lead to perfectly round ends for one-line elements (like most headers and links). A value of `.5em` will create a button shape like the ones common in most operating systems.

Although the attribute is called `border-radius`, it does not require a border to be defined.

Note that there are variations of each tag to support specific corners: `border-top-left-radius` and so on. This can be useful if you do not want to apply the same radius to all four corners of your element.

This attribute is not supported in its default format in any major browsers. However, all the major browsers except IE have vendor-specific variants. Use `-moz-border-radius`, `-webkit-border-radius`, or `-o-border-radius` to get a rounded corner in any of these browsers.

Shadows

You can add a shadow to any element with the `box-shadow` attribute. This tool works much like the `text-shadow` attribute. (**See** "Downloadable Fonts and Text Support" earlier in this part.) The following code adds an attractive drop shadow to a div containing the class `shadow`:

```
.shadow {
  box-shadow: 10px 10px 10px #000000;
  -moz-box-shadow: 10px 10px 10px #000000;
  -webkit-box-shadow: 10px 10px 10px #000000;
}
```

Figure 6-5 illustrates this drop shadow.

Figure 6-5

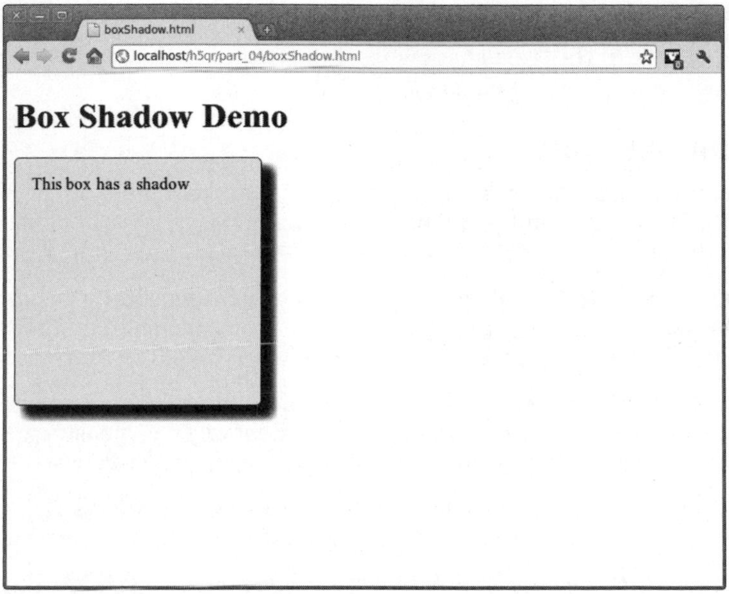

The shadow attribute takes four parameters:

- ✔ **x-offset:** This determines how far the shadow is offset from the main element in the x (left-right) axis. Positive values move the shadow to the right; negative values move the shadow to the left.

- ✔ **y-offset:** This determines how far the shadow is offset from the main element in the y (up-down) axis. Positive values move the shadow downward, and negative values move the shadow up.

- ✔ **cast-length:** This indicates the level of blur of the shadow. A larger value makes the shadow more blurry. A smaller value casts a sharper shadow.

- ✔ **color:** The final parameter is the shadow color. Normally this is black or gray, but you can use other colors to add interesting features.

Like many other CSS3 elements, support for the standard version of box-shadow is spotty (only Opera supports it directly) but vendor-specific variants are available for browsers based on WebKit and Mozilla.

Generally all the shadows on a page should have the same general characteristics. It's most efficient to create a shadow class and add this class to all elements that will have a shadow.

If the original image has rounded corners (*see* the `border-radius` attribute in the "Rounded corners" section, earlier in this part, for details on how to achieve this effect), the shadow will also have rounded corners.

See the example in the "text-shadow" section, earlier in this part, for information on adding shadows to text elements.

Transformations

CSS3 includes the ability to apply geometric transformations onto any element. This provides a remarkable level of visual control not previously available to Web developers.

The `transform` attribute allows you to apply a mathematical transformation to any div. When you apply `transform` to an element, you need to apply one or more of the following parameters to describe the type of transformation:

- **translate:** Moves the object from its default position. Translation requires two parameters, an X measurement and a Y measurement. Use the standard CSS measurement units.

- **rotate:** Rotates the image around its center value and takes one parameter, an angle measurement in degrees. (for example 30 degrees is `30deg`.)

- **scale:** Changes the size of the object. The standard version changes both the horizontal and vertical size uniformly. The `scalex` and `scaley` attributes can be used to adjust the scale along an individual axis. Scale is measured in the standard CSS measurement units. If scale is larger than 1, the object is larger than the original. A scale between zero and one makes the item smaller than it was. Zero or negative scale values are not defined.

- **skew:** This allows you to tilt the element by some angle. The `skew` parameter requires an angle measurement in degrees. The `skewx` and `skewy` variations allow for more complete control of the transformation.

You can combine multiple parameters by listing them after the transform attribute separated by spaces.

To illustrate, imagine the following HTML snippet:

```
<div id = "box1">box 1</div>
<div id = "box2">box 2</div>
<div id = "box3">box 3</div>
<div id = "box4">box 4</div>
<div id = "box5">box 5</div>
```

The code shows five identical divs. For illustration purposes, all the divs share the same common CSS:

```
#box1, #box2, #box3, #box4, #box5{
  width: 100px;
  height: 80px;
  border: 3px solid black;
  background-color: yellow;
}
```

Apply variations of the `transform` attribute to each element to see how the transformations work:

```
#box2 {
  transform: translate(100px, 0px);
}
#box3 {
  transform: rotate(45deg);
}
#box4 {
  transform: scale(2) translate(100px, 0px);
}
#box5 {
  transform: skew(3);
}
```

This code is illustrated in Figure 6-6.

Figure 6-6

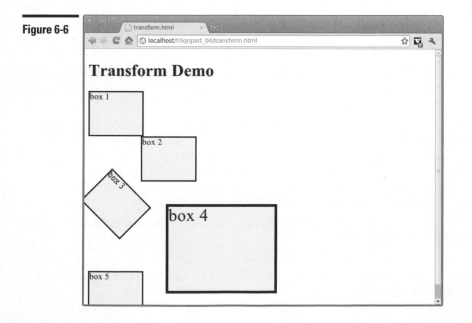

Note that none of the current browsers support the `transform` element as stated in the specifications. However, all of the major browsers except IE have a vendor-specific version, so the actual code for box 2 looks like this:

```
#box2 {
   transform: translate(100px, 0px);
   -webkit-transform: translate(100px, 0px);
   -moz-transform: translate(100px, 0px);
   -o-transform: translate(100px, 0px);
}
```

Transition animation

It's already possible to change CSS properties on the fly through pseudo-classes (like `hover`) or with JavaScript code. Prior to CSS3, all CSS state changes happened instantly. With the new `transition` attribute, you can cause transitions to happen over time.

Look at a simple h1 heading:

```
<h1>Transition Demo</h1>
```

The CSS code is mainly quite straightforward:

```
h1 {
  color: black
  font-size: 300%;
  transition:color 1s ease-in;
}

h1:hover {
   color: red;
}
```

Begin by ignoring the `transition` attribute. If you look at the rest of the code, it's easy to see what it does. In the `normal` state, the heading is black. In the `hover` state, the color is red. Typically, the heading will turn red as soon as the mouse hovers over it, and will instantly turn black when the mouse leaves. However, when the `transition` attribute is added, the color change is not immediate, but takes a second. The color gradually changes from black to red and back.

Transitions are even more interesting when you pair them with transformations. Imagine a very simple div:

```
<div id = "box">Box 1</div>
```

Apply a little CSS3 magic and when the user hovers over the div, it rotates smoothly until it is upside-down. When the user leaves the div, it smoothly rotates back to its original position:

```
#box {
    transition: all 1s ease-in;
    height: 100px;
    width: 100px;
    border: 1px solid black;
}

#box:hover {
    transform: rotate(180deg);
}
```

The `transform` is defined in the `:hover` pseudo-class. The only new element is the transition specified in the class's standard style.

The `transition` attribute takes several parameters:

- ✔ **animation property:** The type of animation defined by this tag. The default value is `all`, but other types are expected to work, including `color`, `length`, `width`, `percentage`, `opacity`, and `number`.

  If in doubt, use the standard `all`.

- ✔ **duration:** The length of the animation in seconds. One second is `1s`.

- ✔ **timing function:** If you want the animation to occur at a constant speed, use `linear`. If you want a more natural motion that gradually speeds up and slows down at the ends of the animation, use one of the following: `ease`, `ease-in`, `ease-out`, `ease-in-out`.

- ✔ **delay:** If you include a second `time` value, this will be considered a delay. The animation will not begin until after the delay.

If you prefer, you can use individual properties for the various parts of the animation, but most developers prefer the one-line shortcut (like the one used for borders).

Not all CSS attributes can be animated, but many can be. It may require some experimentation to determine which CSS attribute can be animated with the `transition` attribute.

Unfortunately, the stock `transition` attribute is not currently supported by any major browsers, but there are vendor-specific versions for Mozilla (`-moz-`), WebKit (`-webkit-`), and Opera (`-o-`). Sadly, there does not appear to be any support for any version of IE yet. Your best bet until support is widespread is to include all vendor-specific versions in addition to the standard version.

Transparency

CSS3 has complete support for adjustable opacity. This is reflected in a couple of ways. First, any element has an `opacity` attribute that can be set from 0 (fully transparent) to 1 (fully opaque.)

Figure 6-7 shows a div with partial transparency superimposed on an image.

The CSS for this effect is quite simple:

```
#box {
  position: absolute;
  top: 350px;
  left: 100px;
  height: 100px;
  width: 100px;
  border: 1px solid red;
  background-color: white;
  opacity: .3;
}
```

All of the code is common CSS2 stuff, except the last attribute. The `opacity` attribute takes a single floating point value between 0 and 1. A value of 0 is completely transparent, and a value of 1 is completely opaque.

Figure 6-7

Part 7

Changes in JavaScript

There are many new features in HTML5, but the biggest change is really in the way that Web pages are used. The Web is no longer simply about hosting documents, but it is becoming an application-development framework. Some of the most interesting and potentially far-reaching innovations in HTML5 are in the new additions to JavaScript available in modern browsers.

JavaScript has emerged as a critical technology for modern Web applications, and every browser has improved the performance of the JavaScript engine in recent years. In addition, a number of fascinating new extensions to the JavaScript language are becoming available.

This part focuses on those aspects of JavaScript that are especially intriguing and new. I assume you have some familiarity with computer programming and the JavaScript language. If you need a refresher, please check my book titled *JavaScript & AJAX For Dummies* (Wiley).

Be sure to check out my Web site for working examples of every code fragment in the book: www.aharrisbooks.net/h5qr.

In this part . . .

✔ **Examining New Selection Options**

✔ **Previewing Data Options**

✔ **Taking a Look at Miscellaneous New JavaScript Features**

Behold: The New JavaScript Selection Options

JavaScript is usually used to interact with the Web page. Generally, the programmer uses the document.getElementById() method to create a variable based on a page element. This mechanism requires the element to have an id attribute. HTML5 incorporates some new ways to select elements from the page.

document.getElementsByClassName()

Sometimes you'll want to apply code to all elements in a particular class. The getElementsByClassName() function returns an array of all the elements in a particular class. For example, look at the following code:

```
function init(){
  specP = document.getElementsByClassName("special");
  alert(specP.length);
  for(i = 0; i < specP.length; i++){
    alert(specP[i].innerHTML);
  } // end for
} // end function
```

This routine creates an array of all of the elements on the current page with the class special. It then steps through each element of that array and alerts the content of that element.

Note that getElementsByClassName() does not return a single element like getElementById(). Instead, it returns an array. Generally, you'll use a for loop to step through the array and do something to each element.

The class does not need to have any CSS associated with it. This can be an easy way to mark a set of elements you'll want to do something with.

document.getElementsByTagName()

The getElementsByTagName() method allows you to quickly retrieve all the elements with a given tag name. For example, you could use this mechanism to get access to all of the input elements of a form. Like getElementsByClassName(), this method returns an array of values (even if there is only one match). You will need to use array syntax (usually with a for loop) to work with the members of the array. The following code alerts the content of every paragraph of the current page:

```
function init(){
  paras = document.getElementsByTagName("p");
  for(i = 0; i < paras.length; i++){
    alert(paras[i].innerHTML);
  } // end for
} // end function
```

document.querySelector()

A number of JavaScript libraries (notably jQuery) have added the ability to select DOM elements through the same syntax used to define elements in CSS. JavaScript now includes this capability natively through the `querySelector()` method. This extremely powerful mechanism makes it very easy to select any element. For example, the following code selects the second paragraph on the page:

```
para2 = document.querySelector("p + p");
alert(para2.innerHTML);
```

 Note that this method retrieves only the first element that matches the query. If the query might match more than one element, use the `document.query-SelctorAll()` method instead. The `querySelector()` method can also be used to select elements by tag name, class, or id.

document.querySelectorAll()

The `document.querySelectorAll()` method works just like `document.querySelector()`, except it retrieves all elements of the page that match the given query. The following function asks for a CSS selector and displays the contents of any page elements matched by that selector:

```
function init(){
  paras = document.getElementsByTagName("p");
  alert(specP.length);
  for(i = 0; i < paras.length; i++){
    alert(paras[i].innerHTML);
  } // end for
} // end function
```

The `querySelectorAll()` method returns an array of elements, even if only a single element is returned. Use array syntax (normally with a `for` loop) to step through each element of the array.

Data Options

Client-side applications (including JavaScript programs) are typically prevented from storing data on the local machine. This is a good thing because it prevents a Web developer from writing malicious code and installing it on your machine. However, this restriction has made it much more difficult to create applications in the browser.

Developers have used server-side solutions (session variables in PHP, persistent data, and so on.) However, the only way to store data on the client has been the cookie mechanism. Cookies are useful, but they are very limited (they allow only

4K of data) – and they are also quite inefficient. (The data is actually passed as part of the HTTP header, and it's passed to the server on every refresh.)

Now that the Web browser is becoming an application platform, it's important to have more robust storage mechanisms that are still safe for the user. There are a couple of very interesting capabilities built into the modern batch of browsers.

Achieving offline cache

Web-based applications are an increasingly important type of application, but they have at least one major problem: Most Web-based applications will work only if you're online. This seems obvious, but it would be nice to have a mechanism for forcing part of a Web page and its resources to be stored on the local machine so that it can be viewed while offline. Of course, many browsers have a save page functionality, but the idea is to have a page identify itself for this behavior and attempt to save a copy on the local machine automatically. The offline cache mechanism serves exactly this purpose. Imagine a page like this:

```
<!DOCTYPE HTML>
<html lang = "en"
      manifest = "cache.manifest">
<head>
  <title>offline.html</title>
  <meta charset = "UTF-8" />
  <link rel = "stylesheet"
        type = "text/css"
        href = "offline.css" />
  <script type = "text/javascript"
          src = "offline.js">
  </script>
</head>

<body onload = "setCaption()">
  <h1>Offline Storage Demo</h1>

  <div>
    <img src = "pot.jpg"
         alt = "hand-etched pottery" />
    <p id = "caption"></p>
  </div>

</body>
</html>
```

While extremely simple, this page manages to draw resources from several different files. Of course, it requires the image pot.jpg, but it also uses an external JavaScript file (offline.js) and an external style sheet (offline.css).

TIP

HTML5 offers a mechanism that allows the browser to automatically save not only the HTML file, but all the other resources it needs to display properly.

I generally wouldn't build such a simple page with so many external dependencies, but that's the point of this particular exercise.

The secret is in a special file called `cache.manifest`. This special file is simply a text file that indicates which other files are needed by the page. Here's the content of `cache.manifest` for this particular example:

```
CACHE MANIFEST
offline.css
offline.js
pot.jpg
```

The file must begin with the phrase CACHE MANIFEST (all in capital letters). Each subsequent line should contain the name of a file needed to complete the page. It's easiest if all the files are in the same directory, but relative references are acceptable.

Here's how you set up a page for offline cache:

1. Set up your server to manage caches. The cache mechanism uses the `text/manifest` MIME type. Your server may not yet be set up for this type of data. If you're using Apache, this is easy to fix. Look for (or create) a text file called `.htaccess` in the root directory of your Web server. Add the following line to this file:

   ```
   AddType text/cache-manifest .manifest
   ```

   If you do not have permission to add or modify `.htaccess` or you are using another server, you might have to ask your server administrator to add this MIME type.

2. Create your manifest file. Build a text file called `cache.manifest` in the same directory as your project. Make the first line read CACHE MANIFEST. On each subsequent line, list one of the assets your page will need. You may need to look through your source code to find the various elements (normally images, CSS, and JavaScript files) that your page will need.

3. Build the page in the normal way. Build your page as you normally do. Keep track of any external resources you might need.

4. Add the manifest attribute to the `<html>` tag. Indicate that your page will request local storage by adding this attribute and a link to your `cache.manifest` file.

5. Load your page. Obviously, you cannot test cache on a local machine (unless you're running your own Web server and test through the `http://localhost` address). You'll need to load your files to a server. The first time you try to access the page, your browser will probably ask permission to save data locally. Grant permission to do so.

6. Test offline. To see if the page works, disconnect from the Internet (by turning off your wireless or unplugging your network cable). Try to load the page again. If you are successful, the entire page including all of its components will load.

Browsers already have a form of cache which automatically stores pages the user has visited, but the type of cache we're building here is a different, more intentional form of cache.

Note that you can't put links to server-side assets in the cache. A local cache can't store a PHP program or database. However, you can use other local storage mechanisms described in this section to store any data you need on the client so your project will still work without a server connection.

If you make changes to your `cache.manifest` file and retest, the browser will not update immediately. That's because browsers are set to keep the current cache for a couple of hours. If you test again after a couple of hours, you will see the changes reflected. During testing, you can turn the automatic browser caching off by adding these lines to your `.htaccess` file:

```
ExpiresActive On
ExpiresDefault "access"
```

It only makes sense to turn off browser caching on a test server. Leave the caching behavior at its default level for a production server.

If one of the files changes but the `cache.manifest` file does not, the browser will not know to reload the changed file. If you want to trigger a complete file reload, you need to change at least one character in the `cache.manifest` file. This can be a comment, so you can just add a version number like this:

```
#version 3
```

Changing the version number will trigger the reload mechanism the next time you're online, so the offline version will be up to date.

Local storage

The local storage mechanism is a nice replacement for cookies. It allows a programmer to write up to 5MB of data to a special file on the client. This file is not executable and cannot hold binary data (only strings), so it's reasonably safe.

All the pages that come from your domain share the same storage area, so you can use this mechanism to keep data persistent between multiple pages. The data also stays on the client machine (until you remove it), so it can be used to keep track of information over time.

The `localStorage` attribute is an example of a very simple (but powerful) type of data structure called a *dictionary*. Each piece of data is stored in a *key/value* pair. The key identifies the name of the information (say 'firstName'), and the value is the value associated with that key ('Herbert'). You've already used dictionaries many times as a Web developer. HTML attributes are dictionaries (in `<a href = "http://www.google.com">`, `href` is the key, and `http://www.google.com` is the value). CSS rules are also dictionaries. (In the style rule `color: red;`, `color` is the key, and `red` is the value.) Some programming languages use different names for dictionaries, including associative arrays and hash tables.

Access to the local storage is through a special built-in object called `localStorage()`. This class has a relatively small number of methods, but they are extremely powerful and easy to use:

- ✔ **`localStorage.setItem(key, value)`:** Stores a value associated with a key. Essentially, `key` is like a variable name, and `value` is the value associated with that key. You can store any type of value you want, but it will be stored as string data.

- ✔ **`localStorage.getItem(key)`:** Retrieves the value associated with the key. Again, you can think of the key as a variable name. Note that this method always returns a string value, so you might need to convert the data to another type. (**See** the counter demonstration later in this section for an example.) If the key does not exist, you will get the special value `null`.

- ✔ **`localStorage.removeItem(key)`:** Removes an item from storage. The key and the value will both be removed. This can be useful if you are running out of space. You are allotted only 5MB of space, and once it's full, nothing else can be added.

- ✔ **`localStorage.length`:** Returns the number of key/value pairs in the database. Usually used in a loop with the `key()` method to work with every key/value pair.

- ✔ **`localStorage.key(i)`:** Given an integer i, this method finds the corresponding key. Note that the order of the keys is not guaranteed. Normally, this method is used in a loop to retrieve all the keys in the database. Then each key is used to look up the corresponding value. See later in this part for an example that pulls all keys and values from `localStorage`.

- ✔ **`localStorage.clear()`:** Clears all key/value pairs from `localStorage`. This is a potentially destructive command, so think carefully before you use it. By definition, `localStorage` data is not backed up on the server (or anywhere else). Once it's gone, it's really gone.

Here's a code snippet that stores and retrieves the user's name:

```
function greet(){
  name = localStorage.getItem("name");
  if (name == null || name == "null"){
```

```
      alert("Hi, Stranger!");
      name = prompt("What is your name?");
      localStorage.setItem("name", name);
    } else {
      alert ("Hi, " + name + "!");
    } // end greet
  } // end function
```

The process is pretty simple:

1. Retrieve the value. Generally, you'll create a variable with the same name as the key. Try to extract the value from the `localStorage` object with the `getItem()` method. Retrieving the data is like checking out a book from the library.

2. Determine if the value exists. If the key does not exist, the value will be `null`. If that's the case, do something to add a value. (I prompted the user for a name.) Note that some browsers look for the value "null" (a string value) and some actually use the keyword `null` (no quotes, because it's a key word). I use the special operator || (or) to check for either possibility.

3. Modify the variable. Your code will likely modify the variable. (In this case, I added a new name from a user prompt.)

4. Store the value back in the database. The `localStorage` database is separated from your variables. It's up to you to update any data you want to keep. Use the `setItem()` method to save data. This is like returning a book to the library.

If you're working with numeric data, you'll need to remember that `localStorage` stores everything as a string. It's no problem to store a numeric value in `localStorage`, but when you retrieve it, you'll need to convert the value back to a numeric value (with `parseInt()` or `parseFloat()`) to the data type you need. Here's an example that counts the number of times a user has visited your site:

```
function countVisits(){
  str_count = localStorage.getItem("count");
  //get a numeric value from str_count, put it in count
  if (str_count == null || str_count == "null"){
    count = 0;
  } else {
    count = parseInt(str_count);
  } // end if

  //increment count
  count++;

  //display count
```

```
lblCounter = document.getElementById("lblCounter");
lblCounter.innerHTML = "You have been here " + count + "
times";

    //store count
    localStorage.setItem("count", count);
} // end count
```

This code would need to be run every time the page is loaded (perhaps with the <body onload> attribute). It works much like the name code, but it involves basic numeric conversions:

1. Attempt to get the count from localStore. Note that I'm storing the counter in a string variable. (JavaScript doesn't require you to specify what type of variable you are using, but they are still different.) I use the str_ prefix to help myself remember that the data is currently a string.

2. Ensure that the value exists. If there is no entry in the database for count, this must be the first time the user is here (or they have cleared the database). In either case, assign the value 0 to count (which is a numeric variable).

3. If str_count exists, convert it to an integer. Use the parseInt() method to convert the string str_count into the integer count.

4. Add one to count. Now that count is an integer, you can add to it.

5. Display the counter value to the user. Of course, this is not absolutely necessary, but it is nice to provide some sort of feedback.

6. Store count back to the localStorage database. Note that you can store the integer count to the database with no problems. It will be quietly converted to a string when it is stored.

It's possible (and easy) to clear any or all of the data. Use the locaStorage. clear() method to clear all of the data associated with your Web site, or the localStorage.removeItem(key) method to remove a particular key/value pair.

```
function clearValues(){
    alert("clearing " + name + " from the database...");
    localStorage.removeItem("name");
    localStorage.removeItem("count");
    //to clear all values at once, you can use this:
    //localStorage.clear();

    //clean up display

    lblCounter = document.getElementById("lblCounter");
```

```
lblCounter.innerHTML = "You have been here 0 times";

}
```

Sometimes, you'll want to step through all the data in the database. This is actu-ally pretty easy to do with the `length` property and the `keys()` method. Look over this example:

```
function viewData(){
  //shows all the key / value pairs

  for (i = 0; i < localStorage.length; i++){
    key = localStorage.key(i);
    value = localStorage.getItem(key);
    alert(key + ": " + value);
  } // end for loop

} // end viewData
```

The process involves creating a `for` loop to step through all the key/value pairs:

1. Build a `for` loop to step through the data. Use the `localStorage.length` property to determine how many times you'll need to step through the loop.

2. Find the next key. Use the loop counter (in my case `i`) to get the next key with `localStorage.key(i)`. Note that the order of the keys will not be predictable.

3. Retrieve the value associated with that key. Use the standard `localStorage.getItem()` method with the key you've just retrieved.

4. Use the key and value. At this point, you have a variable called `key` con-taining the current key, and another called `value` containing the value associated with that key. You can then print out the data to the page or do whatever else you want with it.

If you try to store more than 5MB of data from the same domain, JavaScript will throw a "QUOTA_EXCEEDED_ERR" exception. There is currently no way to change the amount of storage allowed, even with the user's permission.

Amazingly enough, the local storage mechanism works very well on all current browsers, even Internet Explorer.

Of course, any time a Web page can write data to the client machine, there is some concern for privacy and safety. However, the data is stored on the client machine, so it is never transmitted to the server (unlike cookie data). The data is stored on the client machine and belongs to the client. The 5MB limit gives a fair amount of space to Web applications, but even if it is filled, it won't clog up modern machines. Finally, the data is stored in a plain-text format, and it can't be put in a separate file — so it would be difficult to use this technology to create viruses and other troublesome code pests.

It may seem limiting to store data in these simple name/value pairs, but you can actually store very complex data using this mechanism. The value can be any type, including the very rich XML and JSON data storage mechanisms. See a book like *JavaScript & AJAX For Dummies* for help on using these more advanced data structures.

WebSQL database

The `localStorage` mechanism is powerful and easy to use, but most high-end data applications use the relational database model. Typically, the client program connects to a program on the Web server, which then connects to a relational database program like MySQL or Oracle. The server-side program creates a request in a special data language called *SQL* (Structured Query Language). The results of the query are returned to the server, which then sends results back to the client.

If you're interested in more about this model, please see my book *HTML, XHTML, and CSS All-in-One For Dummies* (Wiley). In that book, I explain exactly how to set up this type of a system using the PHP programming language and the MySQL database package.HTML5 introduces a radical new model. The browser actually includes its own database program (based on the popular SQLite engine) and a programmer can build and manage a database directly on the client!

The following SQL code builds a simple database table called `contact` and adds three values to the table:

```
DROP TABLE IF EXISTS contact;
CREATE TABLE IF NOT EXISTS contact (id, name, email);
INSERT INTO contact VALUES(1, 'Andy','andy@aharrisbooks.
net');
INSERT INTO contact VALUES(1, 'Bill', 'bgates@msBob.com');
INSERT INTO contact VALUES(1, 'Steve', 'sJobs@newton.com');
```

The SQL language is powerful and complex. (It deserves a book in its own right.) webSQL features are practical to experiment with only if you're already familiar with standard SQL.

If you want to experiment with the form of SQL used in webSQL, you should look into SQLite (`www.sqlite.org`). This popular database engine is available in many forms. You can download a native version for your platform, or you can use the SQLite manager extension for Firefox. Also, recent versions of Chrome have a database console available. (Right-click anywhere on the page and choose Inspect Element.) The developer tools dialog will appear, and you can use the Storage tab to see any locally-defined databases. If you have a database defined in your page, you can type SQL commands into the console to manage and update the database manually.

Creating a WebSQL database

It's not terribly difficult to create and manage a database through SQL. The first step is to open the database:

```
var db = openDatabase(
 'contact.DB',
 '1.0',
 'Contact DB',
 2 * 1024 * 1024);
```

This powerful command opens a database on the client. It has a number of important parts, including the following:

- **Db handle (**db**):** The openDatabase command will attempt to open a database. It will return a special database object on success, or null on failure. The database object (db in this example) will be used in subsequent database actions.

- **Database name (**contactDB**):** The first parameter is a database name. This will be used internally (for example, browser developer tools) to represent the database.

- **Version number:** This is a place to keep track of the version number of your database. As you change your data structure, you should keep track of version numbers. This will help you manage data as the structure changes. (If possible, you want to avoid changing the data structure after the database is populated.)

- **Display name:** This name might be used to display output tables of the data (although it doesn't seem to be used for anything yet).

- **Storage size in bytes:** The last parameter indicates the amount of storage space you want to allocate for the database. Normally, you'll want to think in megabytes, so 2MB = $2 \times 1024 \times 1024$. (Remember, 1024×1024 bytes is 1MB.)

Once you've created a database, you can start manipulating it. webSQL uses a mechanism called *transactions* to handle database commands cleanly. Essentially, a series of SQL commands are expressed together in a bundle called a *transaction*. The init() method of my example (automatically called with <body onload>) runs two transactions:

```
function init(){
    db.transaction(makeContact);
    db.transaction(getContacts);
} // end init
```

The transaction method of the db object takes a function as its single parameter. Each of these functions (makeContact and getContacts) are described in detail in the next two sections in this part. It's up to the programmer to create the functions to handle the transactions.

Most (virtually all) online examples of WebSQL use an advanced JavaScript technique called *anonymous callback functions*. A *callback* function is a function that will be called at some point during another process. In general, when a callback function is required, you can either present the name of an existing function (as a variable name, with no parameters) or you can create the function you need directly in place.

If you create the function in place, you are building an *anonymous* function. I am not a fan of anonymous functions, particularly for beginners, because they make the code much harder to read. Usually, you are creating an entire function inside a parameter list, making the indentation and bracket notation notoriously confusing. Even though I'm pretty good at anonymous functions, I stay away from them to make my code easier to read and manage.

For that reason, I will not use anonymous functions in the example that follows. Instead, I use a number of standard functions using the callback mechanism. Feel free to use anonymous functions if you're comfortable with them.

Making the contact database

The contact database itself is created through the `makeContact` function. The `db.transaction()` method calls the `makeContact` function. Once the transaction has been created, the browser looks for a function named `makeContact`. Transaction functions are expected to have a single parameter containing a reference to the transaction itself. The transaction object is almost always called `tx`. Here's the code for the complete `makeContact()` function:

```
function makeContact(tx){
tx.executeSql("DROP TABLE IF EXISTS contact");
tx.executeSql("CREATE TABLE IF NOT EXISTS contact
            (id, name, email)");
tx.executeSql(
   "INSERT INTO contact VALUES(1, 'Andy',
   'andy@aharris- books.net')");
tx.executeSql(
   "INSERT INTO contact VALUES(2, 'Bill',
'bgates@msBob. com')");
tx.executeSql(
   "INSERT INTO contact VALUES(3, 'Steve',
   'sJobs@newton. com')");
} // end makeContact
```

Creating the actual database table uses an important method of the transaction object called `executeSql()`. This method accepts an SQL command and passes it to the database.

The code is simply a set of `tx.executeSql()` calls with the various SQL commands for building and populating the database embedded. Each line of SQL is passed to the `executeSql()` command.

If you're using Chrome, you can check the contents of the database with the developer console (right-click on the page, choose Inspect Element, click on the Resources tab, and choose Databases).

There's a variant of the `executeSql()` function that allows you to pass parameters to your requests. For example, this variant passes the variables `id`, `name`, and `email` to the database:

```
tx.executeSql("INSERT INTO contact VALUES(?, ?, ?)",
[id, name, email], null, null);
```

For more information on this four-parameter version of the `executeSql()` method, please read the next section on retrieving output.

Perusing the output of the database

Of course, if you can put data into a database, you'll eventually want to get it out. The general technique is similar. Recall that the `init()` function has the following line:

```
db.transaction(getContacts);
```

This code sets up a second transaction, which is activated by the `getContacts()` function. This function also uses the `tx.executeSql()` command, but in a slightly different way:

```
function getContacts(tx) {
  tx.executeSql('SELECT * FROM contact',
                [],
                showData,
                null);
} // end getContacts
```

The function is technically only one line long, but that line packs a lot. (In fact, I simplified it quite a bit: It's often a lot more convoluted yet.) The `getContacts()` function uses a different variation of `executeSql()` that accepts four parameters:

✔ **Query:** The first parameter is an SQL query. Since the goal of this particular command is to extract data from the database, I use a `SELECT` query. Queries can become much more complex, but they still all work in about the same way.

✔ **Parameters:** You can place an array of string values (enclosed in square braces) to fill in parameters if your query has question mark symbols in it. This works much like a stored procedure in traditional databases, and is a much safer approach than performing string concatenation on the actual SQL code. If you have no parameters, just pass empty square braces ([ ])

✔ **Success callback function:** If the query is successful, call the function named here. The function can be defined elsewhere (in which case only the function name is necessary) or it can be defined in place with an anonymous function definition. If you do not want to use a callback function, use the value null in place of a function name. If you are requesting data from the database, you will need a callback function. In this case, I pass control on to the showData function after a successful query request.

✔ **Failure callback function:** A second callback function can be called if the request is a failure. Typically, this function will report the problem. If you do not want a function to be called, you can use the value null.

Practical considerations of WebSQL

WebSQL sounds like a really great technology, and it is something that developers are pretty excited about. However, it might not be the best technology to use yet. Although it is available now on Safari, Chrome, and Opera, not surprisingly Microsoft is not on board. More shocking is the other holdout. Firefox does not implement WebSQL, and insists it will not support the standard. WebSQL is not formally a part of HTML5 and may not become part of the standard.

Firefox is backing a different variation called *IndexedDB*. At the moment, this is supported only in the gecko-based browsers (Firefox/Mozilla), but the other developers are showing interest. It will be worth watching to see what happens. The localStorage mechanism (*see* "Local storage," earlier in this part) is perfectly fine to use now with modern browsers.

Miscellaneous New JavaScript Features

The HTML5 standard includes a number of other handy features. These are not as easy to categorize, but they do offer impressive new capabilities. Read on to figure out where the browser is, set up notifications, and connect to the server with Web sockets.

Geolocation

Often it's useful to know where the browser is in the world. For mobile apps, this can be especially useful because you can use this information to provide interesting services. For example, you might return search requests that are physically close to the user's location.

Many mobile browsers have access to GPS units on the same machine, which can provide quite accurate position information. Browsers on cellphones can get broad position indication by determining which tower they are getting a signal from, and more precise information by triangulating on multiple towers if they are available. Even a page on a standard desktop machine can provide limited location information by investigating the IP number and other resources.

Up to now, there has not been a standard method to retrieve position information from all these various sources. The new geolocation API is a part of the HTML specification. It provides an easy interface to Web developers so your application can try to determine where exactly the user is.

The basic behavior of this mechanism is a very simple JavaScript call:

```
function getLoc(){
  navigator.geolocation.getCurrentPosition(showMap);
} // end getLoc
```

This function would typically be called from the `body.onload` mechanism or some other initialization script. It calls a single function: `navigator.geolocation.getCurrentPosition()`. The function takes a single argument, which is a callback function. The callback function is the name of a function that should be called as soon as the location has been determined. In my example here, I call the function `showMap()`:

```
function showMap(position){
  var lat = position.coords.latitude;
  var long = position.coords.longitude;
  var linkUrl = "http://maps.google.com?q=" + lat + "," + long;
  var mapLink = document.getElementById("mapLink");
  mapLink.href = linkUrl;
  var embedMap = document.getElementById("embedMap");
  embedMap.src = linkUrl + "&z=16&amp;output=embed";
} // end showMap
```

The `showMap` function is automatically called when the browser has retrieved its location. (The actual method of location discovery is entirely up to the browser and the host hardware; the application doesn't know or care exactly how the location has been retrieved.)

1. Accept `position` object as a parameter. The callback function is always passed a special object called `position`.

2. Extract latitude and longitude from the position. The `position` object has a property called `coords`. This is another object with two properties: `lattitude` and `longitude`. Store those values into local variables for easier handling.

3. Do something with the position data. Latitude and longitude numbers are interesting, but you'll probably want to do something with them. The simplest and easiest thing to do is make a link to Google maps.

4. Build a Google maps link. By digging around on the Google maps page, I was able to figure out how to get a map for any latitude and longitude. Simply make a link to `maps.google.com?q=lat, long`, where `lat` is the latitude, and `long` is the longitude. I used string concatenation to make this link into a string variable. Of course, you aren't limited to Google maps. Just use the latitude and longitude however you want.

5. Make a link to the map. I already have a link on the page. I used standard DOM manipulation techniques to set the `href` property of the link to the derived address.

6. Embed a map. It's also possible to embed a map directly on the page. The result of a Google Maps search includes some 'embed this' code. I simply copied that code and modified it to accept the lattitude and longitude from the current location. Note that the technique shown here uses a technique called the iFrame, which is generally not encouraged. Still, it's cool.

The geolocation API does have some security implications. It allows the page to determine where the browser is in physical space. Of course, the user may not want to disclose this information. Location information is never released without the user's permission. Whenever the user goes to a page that requests location information, the browser pops up a notification that the page is requesting location data. The user can choose to allow or disallow this behavior.

There is much more that can be done with geolocation. For example, you can set up a second function to be called if there is an error getting the position. You can also determine the accuracy of the location. Some kinds of location information (such as GPS) is very precise, where other types (IP) are less precise. It's also possible that a device will use several increasingly accurate types of location, so the accuracy may change over time. (The iPhone uses this technique, finding a very general location first through cell tower location, then eventually spooling up the GPS receiver.)

All major browsers except IE support some form of geolocation. You can use the Google Gears extension to add this capability to IE, or the `geo.js` library from Google (`http://code.google.com/p/geo-location-javascript`) to simplify cross-platform location management.

The `coords` object has a few other properties that may be available (based on your device):

✔ **altitude:** The altitude in meters.

✔ **accuracy:** The accuracy of the current measurement in meters.

✔ **heading:** The direction in degrees the user is traveling.

✔ **speed:** The user's speed in meters per second.

Heading and speed will work only if the browser has been given multiple locations. This is done with the `navigator.geolocation.watchPosition()` function. This function works just like `getCurrentPosition()`. It takes exactly the same parameters (one or two callback functions). The `watch Position()` mechanism calls the callback function whenever the browser has changed position.

Notifications

The notification API is a proposal currently supported in Chrome. It allows the developer to add an operating system–level notification window from the browser. Notifications are something like the old `alert()` box, but they allow a great deal more flexibility.

Like many other advanced JavaScript functions, notifications require user permission. It's necessary to ask the user for permission before popping up notifications.

Here's an example:

```
function notify(){

  if (window.webkitNotifications) {
    //notifications allowed, so proceed...

    //check to see if we have permission from user
    if (window.webkitNotifications.checkPermission() == 0)
{

      //You have permissions
      var note = window.webkitNotifications.
createNotification(
        'andyGoofy.gif',
        'Hi there',
        'This is my notification');
      note.show();
    }else{
      //request permission
      window.webkitNotifications.requestPermission();
      alert("You may need to click the 'notify' button
again");
    } // end "got permission" if

  } else {
    //notifications not supported
```

```
    alert("Notifications are not supported in this browser");

    } // end if

} // end notify
```

Building a notification is similar to many other new JavaScript tools. Here's how it works:

1. Notification must be in response to a user event. I put my notification code in a (cleverly-named) function named `notify`. This function cannot be called with `body onload` or other initialization techniques. Notifications can be activated only in response to direct user actions. This should prevent some of the abuses that occurred when pop-up windows were used as notifications.

2. Check to see if notifications are allowed. Use the `window.webkitNotifications` call to determine whether notifications are supported. Currently, only WebKit supports notifications, so all notification functions have the `webkit` prefix. This will likely be dropped as other browsers incorporate this functionality.

3. See if the user has granted permission to send notifications. Notifications require user permission. If the user has been to this site before (and granted permission), the browser will remember that fact. The `webkitNotifications.checkPermissions()` method returns a numeric code (0 means that permission has been granted).

4. Create the notification. The actual notification will look like a small dialog box outside the browser. Build the actual notification with the `webkitNotifications.createNotification()` method. This method expects three parameters: an image, a text title, and the message to be displayed. Temporarily store the notification in a variable.

5. Display the notification. Use the notification's `show()` method to display the notification to the user.

6. Request permission if necessary. Steps 4 and 5 were executed only if the user has granted permission already. If not, request permission to send notifications using the `webkitNotifications.requestPermission()` method. This will pop up a small dialog asking the user if she is willing to accept notifications. If so, remind users to press the button again, to actually get the notification.

7. If the user's browser does not support notifications, inform her so. It's possible (even likely) that the user's browser does not support notifications. If not, you can fall back on the standard `alert()` box to send information to the user.

The notification mechanism is nice, but it isn't completely necessary. It's possible to send similar information to the user in other ways. This technique is worth keeping an eye on, but currently it isn't terribly useful.

Web sockets

Web sockets are one of the most technically advanced additions to HTML5, and they also have the potential to afford the most dramatic change to the way Internet work is done.

To understand Web sockets, you need to understand how the Web works now. Most Web work is done through the HTTP (HyperText Transfer Protocol). This communication method is quite efficient at sending the kinds of requests that the traditional Internet is based on: The user requests a document, and the server sends it back. HTTP is a *stateless* protocol. That means after a transaction has occurred, the connection between the client and the server is completely broken, and the next transaction will require an entirely new connection. This is a good thing for most applications. Imagine a client goes to your Web page and asks for a form. He looks at it, but decides to go to bed and fill it out in the morning. With stateless HTTP, your server doesn't need to maintain an active connection to that client all night. When the user does decide to submit the form, he'll create a brand-new transaction.

As the Web moves towards an application framework (rather than the document-passing metaphor), the stateless nature of HTTP can become a barrier. One reason AJAX has become so popular is because of how it breaks a large transaction into a series of smaller HTTP requests (often without the user knowing this is happening). This allows for more fluid communication between the client and the server. However, there is still a lot of overhead in creating hundreds of little stand-alone requests.

Long before the Web as we know it, programmers were using an idea called *sockets* to allow remote computers to communicate with a persistent connection. If you've ever used a Telnet, FTP, or SSH client, you've used a program that uses sockets. Typically, the programmer builds two types of sockets: One that lives on the server (a — wait for it — *server socket*) and one that lives on the client. (You're way ahead of me . . . a *client socket.*) These two programs communicate by a predetermined stylized communication agreement, called a *communications protocol.* In fact, Telnet, FTP, HTTP, and many other Internet tools are really more protocols than software. A Telnet program is actually a multipurpose socket client, and it can be used to test many different kinds of server sockets. The Web server itself is a specialized server that mainly speaks HTTP protocol, and the Web browser is a specialized client that speaks HTTP.

You can use a socket tool like Telnet to connect to an HTTP server. To test this, run the following code from the command line. (It should work the same on all major platforms: They all have a basic Telnet program built in.)

```
telnet aharrisbooks.net 80
```

You've connected to the server using port 80 (the standard Web server port). You'll see a response that looks like the following. (Boldface indicates that this comes from the server.)

Trying 66.40.52.176...

Connected to www.aharrisbooks.net.

Escape character is '^]'.

Now the server thinks you're a browser. To get a particular page, you need to send the same request the browser would send. Here's the request needed to get the index for my JavaScript book:

```
GET /jad/index.html HTTP/1.1

host: www.aharrisbooks.net
```

Press the Enter key twice after the last line to submit the request. You'll see a long string of HTML code — all the code that makes up the page. Of course, you'll see only the code because this isn't a real browser. At the end, you'll see this line:

```
Connection closed by foreign host.
```

This always happens because HTTP is a stateless protocol. After every request, the connection is entirely broken.

Web sockets provide an additional protocol. You can still connect to the Web page in the normal way, but when you implement a Web socket, you write code in your Web page that can connect to a server socket and communicate with it. While the page itself still uses the stateless HTTP protocol, the socket connection remains in place as long as the page is active, allowing for complete two-way communication without re-establishing a connection.

The type of connection you get with this mechanism is ideal for applications that require a great deal of client-server communication, such as chat applications and multiplayer games.

Of course, to build a Web socket connection, you need to have both a client and a server. Typically, the server is written in a language like PHP or Python. Here are some examples:

- ✔ **PHP Web socket:** http://code.google.com/p/phpwebsocket/

- ✔ **Python Web socket:** http://code.google.com/p/pywebsocket

Of course, building a server socket requires knowledge of both socket programming and the language the server is built with. Many modern languages support a generic socket mode that can be used to create a specialized Web socket.

Creating a server socket is beyond the scope of this book, so I focus on connecting to an existing server. There's a very nice echo server available at `http://websockets.org/echo.html`.

This simple server simply accepts a message from the client and returns it. Figure 7-1 shows a program that allows the user to input information, which is sent to the server and echoed back.

Figure 7-1

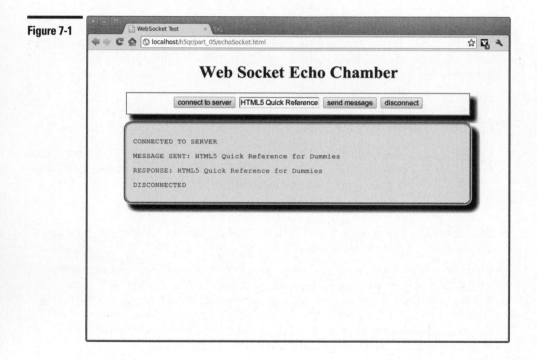

The entire code is somewhat long, but it is still not terribly complicated:

```
<!DOCTYPE HTML>
<html lang = "en">
<head>
<title>WebSocket Test</title>
  <meta charset = "UTF-8" />
  <style type = "text/css">
  h1 {
    text-align: center;
  }

  .error {
    color: red;
```

```
}
.response {
  color: blue;
}

fieldset {
  width: 80%;
  margin: auto;
  text-align: center;
  -moz-box-shadow: 10px 10px 10px #000000;
  -webkit-box-shadow: 10px 10px 10px #000000;
}

#output {
  font-family: monospace;
  width: 80%;
  margin-left: auto;
  margin-right: auto;
  margin-top: 1em;

  background-color: #eeeeee;
  padding: 1em;
  border: 5px groove #cccccc;
  -moz-border-radius: 15px;
  -webkit-border-radius: 15px;

  -moz-box-shadow: 10px 10px 10px #000000;
  -webkit-box-shadow: 10px 10px 10px #000000;
}
</style>
<script language="javascript" type="text/javascript">

var output;
var websocket;

function init(){
  output = document.getElementById("output");
} // end init

function connect(){
  //open socket
  if ("WebSocket" in window){
    websocket = new WebSocket("ws://echo.websocket.org/");
    //note this server does nothing but echo what was passed
```

```
        //use a more elaborate server for more interesting
behavior

      output.innerHTML = "connecting..." ;

      //attach event handlers
      websocket.onopen = onOpen;
      websocket.onclose = onClose;
      websocket.onmessage = onMessage;
      websocket.onerror = onError;
    } else {
    alert("WebSockets not supported on your browser.");
    } // end if

  } // end connect

  function onOpen(evt){
    //called as soon as a connection is opened
    output.innerHTML = "<p>CONNECTED TO SERVER</p>";
  } // end onOpen

  function onClose(evt){
    //called when connection is severed
    output.innerHTML += "<p>DISCONNECTED</p>";
  } // end onClose;

  function onMessage(evt){
    //called on receipt of message
    output.innerHTML += "<p class = 'response'>RESPONSE: "
      + evt.data + "</p>";
  } // end onMessage

  function onError(evt){
    //called on error
    output.innerHTML += "<p class = 'error'>ERROR: "
      + evt.data + "</p>";
  } // end onError

  function sendMessage(){
    //get message from text field
    txtMessage = document.getElementById("txtMessage");
    message = txtMessage.value;

    //pass message to server
    websocket.send(message);
    output.innerHTML += "<p>MESSAGE SENT: " + message + "</
```

```
p>";
  } // end sendMessage

  </script>

</head>

<body onload = "init()">
  <h1>Web Socket Echo Chamber</h1>
  <form action = "">
    <fieldset>
      <button type = "button"
              onclick = "connect()">
        connect to server
      </button>
      <label for = "txtMessage">
        <input type = "text"
               id = "txtMessage"
               value = "HTML5 Quick Reference For Dummies" />
      </label>
      <button type = "button"
              onclick = "sendMessage()">
        send message
      </button>
      <button type = "button"
              onclick = "websocket.close()">
        disconnect
      </button>

    </fieldset>
  </form>

  <div id="output">Click 'connect' button to connect</div>

</body>
</html>
```

Setting up the HTML

As usual, the HTML code in the previous section provides the general framework. In this particular example, I have a simple form with three buttons and an input area:

1. Initialize in `body.onload`. The code will have a small amount of initialization, which will (as usual) be called with the `onload` attribute of the `body` element.

2. Build a Connect button. One button will call a `connect()` function, which will attempt to create the Web socket.

3. Make an Input element for a message. The user will be able to type in a message that will be sent to the browser. Build a simple input element with an associated label for this purpose.

4. Create a "Send Message" button. Another button will be activated when the user is ready to send the current message to the server. This will be attached to a `sendMessage()` function.

5. Build a "Disconnect" button. One more button will close the connection. This code is simple enough that it doesn't require a special function. It's just `websocket.close()`.

6. Create an output area. Use a simple div for output.

7. Style to taste. The default form is a bit dull, so use CSS to clean things up.

Creating the form gives you a pretty good idea what the code will have to do.

Connecting to the socket

If you have a Web socket working (as we do in this example), it's pretty easy to write the JavaScript code to communicate with that socket. The first task is to connect to the socket. You do this by creating a `websocket` object:

1. Check to see if the browser supports Web sockets. The easiest way to do this is by checking to see if the `WebSocket` object is part of the built-in window object.

2. Create a new Web socket. The `new WebSocket()` function creates a connection to a server socket. You must have the URL of a socket that you want to build. For this example, I use the echo server at `echo.web socket.org`. Note that the URL will always begin with `ws` because we're no longer using the default HTTP protocol. For this connection, we're using the new `ws` (Web socket) protocol. Of course, if you create your own server, you'll include the URL to your server here instead.

3. Attach callback methods to the various events. Like standard HTML, the `websocket` object has handles for a number of events. Designate a callback function for each of these events. Sometimes you'll see this done with anonymous functions, but I think it's easier to use standard functions. Of course, you'll have to build each of these functions. (*See* "Creating the callback functions," later in this part).

4. Inform the user if her browser does not support Web sockets. Not all browsers support the Web socket standard yet. The latest versions of Chrome and Firefox 4 support the standard, but IE and Opera lag behind.

Creating the callback functions

In the last step in the previous section, you refer to a number of functions that should be called when various events occur. Of course, those functions need to be created. Most of these functions simply inform the user what is happening. All of the functions are automatically supplied with the parameter `evt`, which is a special object describing what just happened.

- ✔ **onOpen:** When the connection is opened, pass a message to the user indicating a successful connection. I do all output by concatenating onto the `output` element with the `innerHTML` attribute.

- ✔ **onClose:** Likewise, all that needs to happen when the connection is closed is to inform the user.

- ✔ **onMessage:** This function is called when a message has been sent from the server. The content of the message is available in `evt.data`. Pass this information to the user. I chose to change the color of incoming data so it's easy to see what data is coming from the server.

- ✔ **onError:** This function is called when some sort of error has occurred. If an error happened, an explanation of the error is available in `evt.data`. It's wise to somehow mark the error (I put it in red text) to make it obvious that something went wrong.

Sending the message

The user indicates she wants to send a message to the server by clicking the `send message` button. This calls the `sendMessage()` function. This message passes the message to the Web socket object.

Even this process isn't too tough:

1. Extract the message from the text field. In my example, the message is in a text field called `txtMessage`, so I extract that value with ordinary JavaScript code.

2. Pass the message to the `websocket` object. The `websocket` object has a `send()` method.

3. Inform the user the message has been sent. Use the standard mechanism for letting the user know what is going on. When the server responds, the `onMessage()` method will be called automatically.

Some notes about Web sockets

The Web socket protocol is no longer an official part of HTML5, but it is still considered part of the informal HTML5 canon. All major browsers plan to incorporate some form of this feature, but currently only Safari, Chrome and Firefox 4 work.

The real advantage of Web sockets comes with the ability to create a custom server. Web sockets will probably be used most in two scenarios:

- ✔ **Thin client:** In some applications, all the main work should happen on the server, and the client should essentially be an interface. This is an ideal application of Web sockets because the always-open connection provides very quick client-server communication.

- ✔ **Multiuser applications:** When several users want to communicate with each other, they can all talk to a central server. Server sockets will make this easier to manage than the current mechanisms.

Web workers

The Web is rapidly shifting from a document-serving platform to a system for managing applications. However, Web browsers have not been able to take full advantage of modern processors and operating systems.

Essentially, all modern operating systems are *multitasking.* Many computers still have only one CPU (central processing unit — the primary "brain" of the computer). A modern machine with no programs running will often have upwards of 50 processes running in the background. (Use your task manager application to check this on your own machine.) The question is how a single CPU can run all of these programs. Operating systems use a *task-switching* algorithm to switch between various processes and give each program enough CPU time to do its work. Even computers with multiple CPUs (dual-core processors, for example) have the same problem; multiple programs need access to the same limited computing resources. The operating system handles this automatically, and the programmer doesn't normally need to think about it.

Normally, a program occupies a single process in memory, which means it takes its turn along with all the other programs that the OS needs to manage. The Web browser is a program, and it normally occupies a single process. This worked fine when browsers were nothing more than document processors. Now, though, a Web browser acts like an operating system in its own right: It manages applications and programs, which means new kinds of problems can occur.

The problem comes when you ask the browser to do something computationally expensive. For example, assume you want the browser to do something a million times. This is not all that difficult; just use a long `for` loop. However, while that loop is running, that's the only thing the browser can do. There will be no processor power left for managing the interface, responding to the mouse, or anything else. The browser (and sometimes the entire operating system) will appear to lock up while the CPU grinds away on a single problem.

In traditional programming, the solution is to create something called a *thread.* Essentially, this is a new miniprogram that gets its own place in the CPU's to-do list. Create a thread, put the expensive code in the thread, and let the operating system figure out how to run it. Then the main program will not freeze, and the computation will run in the background. If the CPU has multiple cores, the operating system will often be able to take advantage of a separate CPU and use it for the thread.

Until now, Web browsers didn't have a good way to implement threading. The browser and all of its code occupied a single thread, and if you had a computationally expensive problem, you were just out of luck. Most programmers didn't mind, because working with threads can be very tricky. You're always looking for certain problems called *deadlocks* and *race conditions,* so thread programming has long been considered a kind of black art.

HTML5 introduces a fascinating new technology called the *Web worker.* It's an easy and powerful way to add threading capability to your browser. Here's essentially how a Web worker does its magic:

1. Create your page and JavaScript code as usual. Generally, Web workers are used for optimization, so often you'll use them to fix some code that's running slowly. Generally, you isolate a chunk of code that's hogging the CPU (which is often called a *critical section*). That's the code you're going to move to a Web worker.

2. Identify computationally expensive code. Find the code that is hogging CPU resources. Normally, this is a big loop or heavy data initialization. That's the code that's going to be moved to the worker.

3. Create a separate JavaScript file containing the critical section. Build an entirely separate file with the .js extension. This file will hold a function (or perhaps several functions) of code that will benefit from running in a separate thread.

4. In your main page, create a Worker object. This is a special new class. It expects the name of a .js file (normally on the same server as the Web page) as its single parameter. The browser will create a Web worker based on that file, which will have the critical section code in it.

5. Designate a function to run when you receive a message from the worker. Web workers use a *message-passing* algorithm. The worker and the main page are entirely different programs to the CPU. The only way they communicate is by passing messages back and forth. The worker object has an onmessage event handler. Attach a function to this message, and the function will activate every time the main program receives a message from the worker.

6. Pass messages to the worker to tell it what to do. The only way to control the worker is to pass a message to it. The worker object has a postMessage() method. Send a value to this message, and that message will be sent to the worker. Of course, you'll need to set up the worker to receive the message and act accordingly.

7. Give the worker an `onmessage` function. Just like the main page, the worker (which is, remember, just a JavaScript file) can have an `onevent` handler. Attach a function to `onevent`, and the worker will run that function whenever the event is triggered.

8. Write the function code. The worker is an entirely separate program from the main code. It doesn't know about the Web page, or any objects on it. All it knows is the message sent to it. All it can do (apart from any calculations or processing) is send a message back. However, that's all we need for most processing.

9. Destroy the `Worker` object when you're finished. A Web worker takes up CPU time, so you'll need to terminate it when you're done with it — or it will stay in memory. The worker has a `terminate()` method that requests the worker to commit glorious seppuku.

The easiest way to see it in action is to look at a simple example. Take a look at the following HTML code:

```
<body>
  <h1>Web worker demo</h1>
  <button onclick = "startWorker()"
          type = "button">
    start web worker
  </button>
  <button type = "button"
          onclick = "stopWorker()">
    stop web worker
  </button>

  <div id = "output">
    default output
  </div>
</body>
</html>
```

This page is nothing more than a couple of buttons that call `startWorker()` and `stopWorker()`. There's also a div for output, which will show the output of any calculations.

This page is going to count from zero to 100,000. Depending on the speed of your CPU and which browser you use, this problem can take a minute or more. Without Web workers, your browser would freeze during the loop. However, my code won't actually run the loop. Instead, it creates a separate Web worker, which runs the loop in an entirely new process. Here's the JavaScript code (embedded in the head of the page, as usual):

```
//set up global vars
var worker;
var output;

function startWorker(){

  //initialize worker
  worker = new Worker("worker.js");
  output = document.getElementById("output");

  //when we get a message from worker, run update function
  worker.onmessage = update;

  //tell worker to get started
  worker.postMessage("start");
} // end init

function update(evt){
  //update the page with current message from worker
  output.innerHTML = evt.data;
} // end update

function stopWorker(){
  //stop the worker
  worker.terminate();
} // end stopWorker
```

Although we're doing somewhat advanced programming here, the actual code is quite simple. Here's how to set this up:

1. Build some global variables. I'll need access to a special `Worker` object (which I'll call `worker`) and the `output` element throughout the code. As usual, any variables that will be used in multiple functions should be declared outside any functions.

2. Create three functions. My code uses three functions (on the Web page — there will be more later). The `startWorker` function happens when the user clicks the `start worker` button. The `stopWorker` function happens when the user clicks the `stop worker` button. (I love naming conventions.) The `update` function will be called when the main program receives a message from the worker.

3. Designate a function to run when the worker sends a message. When the worker sends a message, a special function will be run. Use the `worker.onmessage` designator to specify which function will run when a message is received. In my example, I will call the `update()` method (described in Step 5) whenever my program receives a message from the worker. This is normally done in the initialization function.

4. Pass a message to the worker. The only way to communicate with the worker is to pass a message to it. A message is simply some sort of value. The `worker.postmessage()` function lets you send a message to the worker. I simply send the string `"start"` in this case. Later when I create the worker, I'll need to tell it how to respond to the start message.

5. Write the `update()` function. In Step 3, I specified that whenever the page receives a message from the worker, it should run a function called `update()`. Of course, this means I should *have* a function called `update`. The callback function of a Web worker is automatically passed a single parameter that describes the event that occurred. I call that object `evt`.

6. Print any messages coming from the worker. If a message comes from the worker, copy that message to the `innerHTML` of the `output` object. The `evt.data` element contains the message sent from the worker.

7. Stop the worker when requested. If the user wants to stop the worker, the `stopWorker()` function does the job. It simply calls the worker's `terminate()` method, which destroys the worker.

So far, you've only built the Web page part of the system. The Web worker is a separate file. Fortunately, it's really easy to build. Any JavaScript code inside a text file with the `.js` extension can be a Web worker. The Web worker will be run by the operating system as a completely separate program from the browser, which means it will not block the browser from doing other things. However, the code in a worker is not related to the browser or the page, so it cannot interact directly with the page. All of its input comes from messages passed from the browser, and all the output is messages passed to the browser. The worker cannot work with the local document (because as far as it knows, there *is no* local document).

Here's my simple Web worker (stored in `worker.js`):

```
//tell system to runloop when a message comes in
onmessage = runLoop;

function runLoop(evt){
   if ( evt.data === "start" ) {
      for(i = 0; i < 100000; i++){
         postMessage(i);
      } // end for
```

```
        //send a message showing we're done
        postMessage("finished");
    } // end if
} // end runLoop
```

The worker is ordinary JavaScript, but it uses the message mechanism to communicate with the page:

1. Run the `runLoop()` function when a message is received. Use the `onmessage` mechanism to tell the program to run the `runLoop()` function whenever a message comes to the worker.

2. Build the `runLoop()` function. This function automatically passes an event object as its single parameter.

3. Check to see if the incoming message is `"start"` or not. The way this particular example is written, there is only one incoming message. Often there may be a number of different messages that come in from the browser. You'll typically need to look at the incoming event to see what it is your program should be doing.

4. Begin a computationally expensive process. For this example, I have the worker count to 100,000 in a `for` loop. This is a long enough process that it would temporarily freeze the browser if it were done in an ordinary JavaScript function. Because the loop is happening in a separate thread, the browser will generally not slow down at all.

5. Pass the current counter back to the browser. You can use the `postmessage()` method to send some kind of information back to the browser. In this example, I pass the current counter back to the browser. This will trigger the browser's `update()` function, which will in turn update the output area.

6. Pass another message indicating the process is finished. This isn't necessary, but it can be nice. Doing so gives your main program a way of knowing that the process is done — and the worker can be terminated or other work that depended on the worker can begin.

Part 8

Working with the Canvas

The canvas element is one of the most interesting new developments in HTML5. While the `<canvas>` tag is an HTML tag, it really isn't interesting without JavaScript programming. The `canvas` tag provides a *graphics context,* which is an area of the page that can be drawn upon with JavaScript commands.

Canvas supplies a rich toolkit of drawing operations that may very well revolutionize the Web. Innovations in the canvas tag — along with advances in the speed of JavaScript engines — may very well lead to new uses of the Web. A number of developers have developed games with the canvas tag and JavaScript that would have required Flash or Java just a few years ago. Also, the flexibility of canvas could lead to entirely new visual tools and widgets that are not based on HTML, which could have profound implications on usability and user interfaces.

The canvas tag is supported by nearly all current browsers. The latest versions of Chrome, Safari, Opera, and Firefox all support the canvas tag elements completely. (To be honest, pixel-level manipulation is not available in Firefox 3.x, but is in Firefox 4.) The one notable holdout is (you probably guessed it) Microsoft. As of IE8, the canvas tag is still not supported, although support for the canvas element is promised for IE9. In the meantime, the *ExplorerCanvas* project available at `http://excanvas.sourceforge.net` is a promising alternative. It allows an easy way to add canvas functionality to even the older versions of IE.

Although many of the features of the canvas element (shadows, transformations, and images) are available through other parts of the HTML5 universe, the implementation of the various canvas elements is identical on all browsers that support the platform.

Be sure to check out my Web site for working examples of every code fragment in the book: `www.aharrisbooks.net/h5qr`.

In this part . . .

- ✔ Examining Canvas Basics
- ✔ Previewing Fill and Stroke Styles
- ✔ Creating Primitive Shapes
- ✔ Drawing Complex Shapes
- ✔ Using Images
- ✔ Adding Transformations
- ✔ Implementing Animation
- ✔ Taking a Look at Pixel Manipulation

Canvas Basics

Begin with a simple demonstration of the canvas tag. The canvas variation of "Hello World" creates a simple canvas and draws a rectangle on it.

Setting up the canvas

To use the canvas tag, build a Web page with a `canvas` element in it. Typically, you'll provide `width`, `height`, and `id` parameters:

```
<canvas id = "drawing"
        width = "200"
        height = "200">
  <p>Your browser does not support the canvas tag...</p>
</canvas>
```

Inside the canvas tag, you can put any HTML code you want. This code will appear if the browser does not support the canvas tag. Typically, you'll just put some sort of message letting the user know what she's missing.

Nothing interesting happens in a canvas without some kind of JavaScript code. Often, you'll use a function to draw on the screen. Here's my `draw()` function, which is called by the `body onload` event:

```
function draw(){
  var canvas = document.getElementById("drawing");
  if (canvas.getContext){
    var con = canvas.getContext('2d');
    con.fillStyle = "#FF0000";
    con.fillRect(10, 10, 50, 50);
  } // end if
} // end draw
```

The `draw()` function illustrates all the main ideas of working with the canvas tag. Here's how you build a basic drawing:

1. Create a variable reference to the canvas. Use the standard `getElement ById()` mechanism to create a variable referring to the canvas.

2. Extract the graphics context from the canvas. Canvas elements have a *graphics context,* which is a special object that encapsulates all the drawing methods the canvas can perform. Most browsers support a 2D context now, but 3D contexts are planned.

3. Set the context's `fillStyle`. The `fillStyle` indicates how you will color filled-in areas (like rectangles). The basic approach is to supply a CSS-style color value. *See* "Controlling Fill and Stroke Styles," later in this part, for information on how to fill with colors, gradients, or image patterns.

4. Create a filled-in rectangle. The graphics context has a few built-in shapes. The rectangle shape is pretty easy to build. It expects four parameters: x, y, `width`, and `height`. The x and y parameters indicate the position of the rectangle's top-left corner, and the `width` and `height` parameters indicate the size of the rectangle. All measurements are in pixels. See "Drawing Essential Shapes," later in this part, for more information on the various types of primitive shapes you can build.

Understanding how canvas works

I go into detail throughout this part, but it's helpful to begin with an overview of the way canvas works and what it does in general.

There are really only two main drawing functions in canvas: fill and stroke. Most drawing is done as a two-step process. First, you define some sort of shape (a rectangle, an arc, a series of lines), and then you tell the canvas to draw with a *stroke* or a *fill*. A stroke simply draws a line — so if you stroke a rectangle, you'll see the outline of the rectangle, but it will not be filled in. The fill draws the filled-in shape, so a filled rectangle will show the interior of the rectangle.

You can specify a *fillStyle,* which specifies the color and pattern of subsequent fill commands. You can also indicate a *strokeStyle,* which determines how subsequent stroke commands will be drawn.

More complex shapes are drawn with a mechanism called *paths,* which are a series of line-drawing instructions. You can use paths to create strokes or filled-in shapes.

You can draw images onto a canvas. You can draw an entire image, or part of an image, onto the canvas.

You can also draw text directly onto the canvas in various fonts and colors. You can add shadow effects to your text elements, or even images.

The canvas object gives you access to the underlying data of an image. This allows you to perform any kind of transformation you want on image data, including color balancing, adjusting brightness, and so on.

It's possible to add *transformations* to any of your objects. Transformations allow you to move, resize, or rotate any element (text, drawing, or image) you place on the canvas.

Finally, you can use JavaScript's animation and user-interface tools to build your own animations that move an element around in real time or under user control.

Controlling Fill and Stroke Styles

Nearly every operation in the canvas implements a fill or stroke style. To get the most out of canvas, you need to understand how they work. There are three primary types of styles that can be used on fills and strokes: colors, gradients, and patterns.

Colors

There are a number of places where you can indicate a color value in the canvas API. In general, you can use the same color tools you use in CSS and HTML:

✔ **Six-digit hex values:** The most common way to manage colors is with the same six-digit hexadecimal scheme commonly used in CSS, with two digits each for red, green, and blue. The value begins with a pound sign. For example, #FF0000 is red, and #FFFF00 is yellow.

✔ **Three-digit hex values:** Hex color values often use repeating values, so you can abbreviate these values as three-digit numbers. In this scheme, red is #F00, and yellow is #FF0

✔ **Color names:** You can often use color names, like "red" or "yellow." Common color names will usually work, but not all browsers support the same list of color names, so "papaya whip" is not likely to be supported. (It sounds more like a desert recipe than a color to me anyway.)

✔ **RGB and RGBA values:** You can use the rgb() function to create colors using integers (0–255) or percentages (0%–100%). Red would be rgb(255, 0, 0), and yellow is rgb(100%, 100%, 0%). Note that the rgb function must go in quotes like any other color value. If you want to include alpha, add a fourth parameter, which is a zero-one value. Transparent red would be rgba(255, 0, 0, 0.5).

✔ **HSL and HSLA:** The new hsl and hsla color formats are supposed to be supported by the canvas element, but so far, the support for these features varies by browser.

Note that the various values for a color are always enclosed in quotes. The color parameter is a string that can be interpreted as a CSS color.

Gradients

You can also fill a shape with a gradient. Canvas gradients are defined in two steps:

✔ **Create a gradient object.** There are two methods built into the context object for this. One builds linear gradients, and the other builds radial gradients.

✔ **Add color stops.** A *color stop* is a special element that indicates a color to be added to the gradient. You can add as many colors as you want, and you can also specify where along the gradient pattern the color will appear.

The following code builds a radial gradient and a linear gradient on a canvas:

```
function draw(){
  var drawing = document.getElementById("drawing");
  var con = drawing.getContext("2d");

  //build a linear gradient
  lGrad = con.createLinearGradient(0,0,100,200);

  lGrad.addColorStop(0, "#FF0000");
  lGrad.addColorStop(.5, "#00FF00");
  lGrad.addColorStop(1, "#0000FF");

  con.fillStyle = lGrad;
  con.fillRect(0, 0, 100, 200);

  //build a radial gradient
  rGrad = con.createRadialGradient(150, 100,
        0, 150, 100, 100);
  rGrad.addColorStop(0, "#FF0000");
  rGrad.addColorStop(.5, "#00FF00");
  rGrad.addColorStop(1, "#0000FF");

  con.fillStyle = rGrad;
  con.fillRect(100,0, 200, 200);


} // end draw
```

The output of this code is shown in Figure 8-1.

A *linear* gradient is a pattern of colors that blend into each other along a straight-line path. To define a linear gradient, follow these steps:

1. Create a variable to hold the gradient. Gradients are a little more complex than simple colors, so they are stored in variables to be reused.

2. Build the gradient. Use the createLinearGradient() method of the context object to build a linear gradient.

Figure 8-1

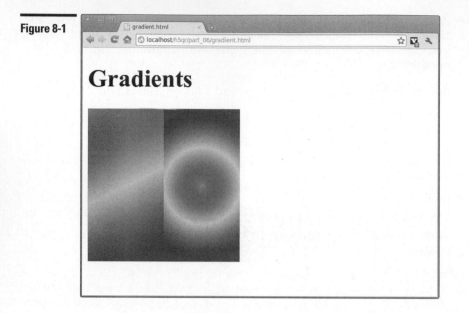

3. Define the gradient path. The createLinearGradient() method expects four parameters. These define a line (x1, y1, x2, y2). The colors will be perpendicular to this line, so if you want horizontal color bands, draw a vertical line. If you want vertical color bands, draw a horizontal line. In my example, I drew a diagonal line for diagonal colors. The line typically takes up the entire width or height of the element, but it does not have to. If the line is smaller than the image, the excess area will be automatically assigned a color from the nearest end of the gradient.

4. Add color stops. Gradients aren't much fun without colors. The add ColorStop() method of the gradient object allows you to add a color to the gradient. Each color stop has two parameters: position and color. The position is a 0–1 value indicating where on the gradient line the color should be positioned. 0 is the beginning, 1 is the end, and intermediate values are in the middle. The color parameter is a text value that can be evaluated as a CSS color. (You can use any of the mechanisms described in the preceding section.) At a minimum, you should define two color stops, one for the beginning and one for the end.

5. Apply the gradient as a fill pattern. If you want to use the gradient as a fill pattern, set the context's fillStyle to the gradient variable you just created. All subsequent fills will be done using the gradient pattern (until the fillStyle is changed to something else).

Radial gradients are similar. Rather than drawing a gradient in a straight line, they draw a series of circular color bands. The first color is the center of the circle, and the last color defines an outer radius. Building a radial gradient is very similar to building a linear gradient. The only difference is the create command.

Use the console object's createRadialGradient() method to build a radial gradient. This command actually takes six parameters:

- **beginX:** The X position of the starting point. This is often in the center of your shape.

- **beginY:** Along with beginX, this determines the beginning position of your gradient.

- **beginRadius:** The radius of your center circle. Usually this is zero, but you can make it larger if you want to emphasize the center color more.

- **endX:** Describes the X position of the ending circle. Typically, this is the same as beginX.

- **endY:** Along with endX, defines the position of the ending circle. If the beginning and ending circles have the same positions, you'll get a circular gradient. Change the ending position to make the gradient stretch in a particular direction.

- **endRadius:** The ending radius defines where the last color gradient will be placed. Smaller values for this radius will lead to a tightly grouped gradient, and larger values will spread the gradient along a larger area.

Once the gradient is defined, the addColorStops() method works exactly like it does for linear gradients. The variable created through the addRadial Gradient() command is usually stored in a variable, where it can be used for subsequent fillStyle() requests.

Patterns

A *pattern* is used to define an image to be used as a fill or stroke. You can use any image as a pattern, but it's generally best to find or create an image that is designed to be tiled. (Check out my book, *HTML, XHTML, & CSS All-in-One For Dummies, 2nd edition,* for complete information on how to build tiled patterns using free software.)

There are many sources of tiled patterns available on the Web as well. Once you've got an image you want to use as a fill pattern, here's how to implement it in the canvas tag:

```
function draw(){
  var drawing = document.getElementById("drawing");
  var con = drawing.getContext("2d");
```

```
var texture = document.getElementById("texture");

pFill = con.createPattern(texture, "repeat");
con.fillStyle = pFill;

con.fillRect(10,150,190,150);

con.font = "40px sans-serif";
con.fillText("Pattern!", 20, 80);

con.strokeStyle = pFill;
con.lineWidth = 5;
con.strokeRect(10, 10, 180, 100);

} // end draw
```

You can see the results of this code in Figure 8-2.

Figure 8-2

A pattern is simply an image. Building a pattern is relatively straightforward:

1. **Get access to an image.** You'll need a JavaScript image object to serve as the basis of your pattern. There are a number of ways to do this, but the easiest is to create the image somewhere in your HTML, hide it with the display:none style, and use the standard document.getElementById()

technique to get access to your image. (*See* "Images," later in this part, for alternate ways to load images.)

2. Create a variable for the pattern. Like gradients, pattern fills can be reused, so store the pattern in a variable for later reuse.

3. Build the pattern. The context's `createPattern()` method creates a pattern from an image.

4. Specify the pattern's repeat parameter. The second parameter indicates how the pattern will repeat. The default value is `"repeat"`, which repeats the pattern in both the X and Y axes indefinitely. If your pattern is not tiled, you will see a visible seam where the pattern repeats. You can also set the repeat value to `reapeat-x`, `repeat-y`, and `no-repeat`.

5. Apply the pattern variable to the `fillStyle` or `strokeStyle`. Assign the pattern variable to the context's `fillStyle` (or `strokeStyle`) and then perform any fill operation to draw in the pattern.

Drawing Essential Shapes

A few primitive shapes can be drawn directly onto the graphics context. The most common shapes are rectangles and text, which can also have shadows.

Drawing rectangles

You can draw three different types of rectangles:

- ✔ **clearRect(x, y, w, h):** Erases a rectangle with the upper-left corner (x, y) and size (w, h). Generally, erasing will draw in the background color.

- ✔ **fillRect(x, y, w, h):** Draws a box with upper-left corner (x, y) and size (w, h). The rectangle is filled in with the currently defined `fillStyle`.

- ✔ **strokeRect(x, y, w, h):** Draws a box with upper-left corner (x, y) and size (w, h). The box is not filled in, but the outline is drawn in the currently-defined `strokeStyle` and using the current `lineWidth`.

Figure 8-3 illustrates a few rectangles.

Here's the code that generates Figure 8-3.

```
function draw(){
  var drawing = document.getElementById("drawing");
  var con = drawing.getContext("2d");

  con.fillStyle = "red";
  con.strokeStyle = "green";
```

```
    con.lineWidth = "5";

    con.fillRect(10, 10, 180, 80);
    con.strokeRect(10, 100, 180, 80);

} // end draw
```

Figure 8-3

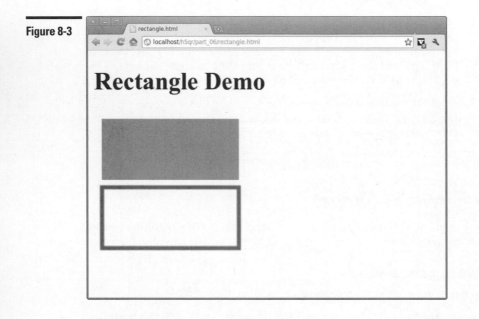

Drawing text

The canvas tag has complete support for text. You can add text anywhere on the canvas, using whichever font style and size you want.

Figure 8-4 shows a canvas with embedded text.

Text is drawn onto the canvas much like a rectangle. The first step is to pick the desired font. Canvas fonts are created by assigning a font to the context's `font` attribute. Fonts are defined like the single-string font assignment in CSS. You can specify all the font characteristics in the same order you do when using the font shortcut: style, variant, weight, size, and family.

When you're ready to display actual text on the screen, use the `fillText()` method, which accepts three parameters. The first parameter is the text to display. The last two parameters are the X and Y position of the left-hand side of the text. The following code is used to produce the result shown in Figure 8-4:

```
function draw(){
  var drawing = document.getElementById("drawing");
  var con = drawing.getContext("2d");

  //clear background
  con.fillStyle = "white";
  con.fillRect(0,0, 200, 200);

  // draw font in red
  con.fillStyle = "red";
  con.font = "20pt sans-serif";
  con.fillText("Canvas Rocks!", 5, 100);
  con.strokeText("Canvas Rocks!", 5, 130);

} // end draw
```

Figure 8-4

Enhancing shapes with shadows

You can add shadows to anything you draw on the canvas. Shadows are quite easy to build. They require a number of methods of the `context` object:

✔ **shadowOffsetX:** Determines how much the shadow will be moved along the X axis. Normally, this will be a value between zero and 5. A positive value moves the shadow to the right of an object. Change this value and the `shadowOffsetY` value to alter where the light source appears to be.

- ✔ **shadowOffsetY:** Determines how far the shadow is moved along the x axis. A positive value moves the shadow below the object. In general, all shadows on a page should have the same X and Y offsets to indicate consistent lighting. The size of the offset values implies how high the element is "lifted" off the page.

- ✔ **shadowColor:** Indicates the color of the shadow. Normally, this is defined as black, but the color can be changed to other values if you want.

- ✔ **shadowBlur:** The shadowBlur effect determines how much the shadow is softened. If this is set to zero, the shadow is extremely crisp and sharp. A value of 5 leads to a much softer shadow. Shadow blur generally lightens the shadow color.

If you apply a shadow to text, be sure that the text is still readable. Large simple fonts are preferred, and you may need to adjust the shadow color or blur to ensure the main text is still readable.

Once you've applied shadow characteristics, all subsequent drawing commands will incorporate the shadow. If you want to turn shadows off, set the shadow Color to a transparent color using RGBA.

Here's the code to produce text with a shadow:

```
function draw(){
  var drawing = document.getElementById("drawing");
  var con = drawing.getContext("2d");

  //clear background
  con.fillStyle = "white";
  con.fillRect(0,0, 200, 200);

  // draw font in red
  con.fillStyle = "red";
  con.font = "20pt sans-serif";

  //add shadows
  con.shadowOffsetX = 3;
  con.shadowOffsetY = 3;
  con.shadowColor = "black";
  con.shadowBlur = 5;
  con.fillText("Canvas Rocks!", 5, 100);

} // end draw
```

Drawing More Complex Shapes

More complex shapes are created using the path mechanism. A *path* is simply a series of commands played back by the graphics context. You can think of it as a recording of pen motions. Here's an example that draws a blue triangle with a red border:

```
function draw(){
  var drawing = document.getElementById("drawing");
  var con = drawing.getContext("2d");

  con.strokeStyle = "red";
  con.fillStyle = "blue";
  con.lineWidth = "5";

  con.beginPath();
    con.moveTo(100, 100);
    con.lineTo(200, 200);
    con.lineTo(200, 100);
    con.lineTo(100, 100);
  con.closePath();
  con.stroke();
  con.fill();
} // end draw
```

The code shown here generates the output displayed in Figure 8-5.

Figure 8-5

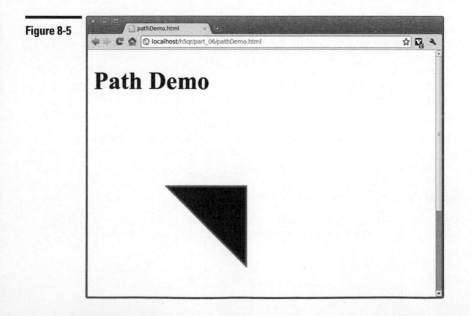

The technique for drawing a path is not terribly complicated, but it does involve new steps.

1. Generate the graphics context. All `canvas` programs begin by creating a variable for the canvas and another variable for the graphics context.

2. Set the stroke and fill styles. The stroke style indicates the color of lines. The `lineWidth` attribute describes how wide the line will be (in pixels), and the fill style indicates the color that enclosed shapes will have.

3. Begin the path. A path is a series of drawing commands. Use the `begin Path()` method to start your path definition.

4. Move the pen. The `moveTo(x,y)` command moves the pen to a particular point on the screen without drawing.

5. Draw lines. The `lineTo(x, y)` command draws a line from the current pen position to the indicated `(x, y)` coordinates. (*See* "Making arcs and circles," "Making quadratic curves," and "Producing a bezier curve," later in this part, for information on other drawing commands.)

   Note that the line will still not be visible. See Step 7.

6. Close the path. When you're finished with a path, use the `closePath()` function to indicate you are finished defining the path.

7. Stroke or fill the path. When you define a path, it is not immediately displayed! The `stroke()` command draws a line using the current stroke style and line width along the path. If you prefer, use the `fill()` command to draw a filled-in shape defined by the path. If the path did not define a closed shape, the `fill()` command will draw a line from the ending point to the beginning point. The `fill()` command fills in the path with the color, gradient, or pattern designated with `fillStyle()`.

Note that the `closePath()` function draws a connecting line between the first point of the path and the last point. This will create closed shapes. If you want a path to remain open, use the `stroke()` command before the `closePath()` command. It is still necessary to call `closePath()` before creating a new path.

The `lineTo()` method doesn't actually draw a line! It simply indicates your path. The path is not visible until you execute a `stroke()`, `closePath()`, or `fill()` command.

Line-drawing options

Whenever you are using stroke commands, you can modify the line width and style with a number of interesting options. Figure 8-6 shows a few of these choices.

Figure 8-6

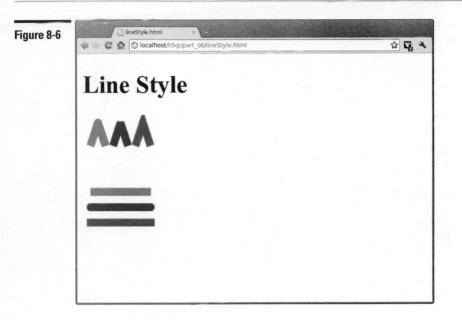

Here's the code used to create Figure 8-6:

```
function draw(){
  var drawing = document.getElementById("drawing");
  var con = drawing.getContext("2d");

  //change line width and color
  con.strokeStyle = "red";
  con.lineWidth = 10;

  con.lineJoin = "round"
  con.beginPath();
  con.moveTo(10, 40);
  con.lineTo(20, 10);
  con.lineTo(30, 40);
  con.stroke();
  con.closePath();

  con.strokeStyle = "blue";
  con.lineJoin = "bevel"
  con.beginPath();
  con.moveTo(40, 40);
  con.lineTo(50, 10);
  con.lineTo(60, 40);
```

```
        con.stroke();
        con.closePath();

        con.lineJoin = "miter";
        con.strokeStyle = "green"
        //draw a simple line
        con.beginPath();
        con.moveTo(70, 40);
        con.lineTo(80, 10);
        con.lineTo(90, 40);
        con.stroke();
        con.closePath();

        //line caps
        con.lineCap = "butt";
        con.strokeStyle = "red"
        con.beginPath();
        con.moveTo(10, 100);
        con.lineTo(90, 100);
        con.stroke();
        con.closePath();

        con.lineCap = "round";
        con.strokeStyle = "blue"
        con.beginPath();
        con.moveTo(10, 120);
        con.lineTo(90, 120);
        con.stroke();
        con.closePath();

        con.lineCap = "square";
        con.strokeStyle = "green"
        con.beginPath();
        con.moveTo(10, 140);
        con.lineTo(90, 140);
        con.stroke();
        con.closePath();

    } // end draw
```

While the code is long, it is quite repetitive. There are only a few new elements:

- **strokeStyle:** Use any of the style options (color, gradient, or pattern) to specify how your line will be drawn.

- **linewidth:** Specify the width of your line in pixels.

- ✔ **lineJoin:** The `lineJoin` property indicates how corners will be rendered in your paths. The default form is `"miter"` (which produces sharp corners). You can also choose `"round"` (which gives rounded corners) and `"bevel"` (which squares off the corners).

- ✔ **lineCap:** You can also determine how the ends of the lines are rendered. Use `"round"` to produce rounded edges, `"square"` to produce squared-off edges, and `"butt"` to produce edges that are cut off exactly at the line width. Square and butt look almost identical, but square adds a small length to each line, and butt cuts off the line immediately.

Making arcs and circles

Arcs and circles are part of the `path` mechanism. They are created much like lines, as they are executed as part of a path. Once the path is complete, use the `stroke()` or `fill()` command to actually draw the arc or circle.

Arcs and circles are both created with the `arc()` method.

To draw an arc or a circle:

1. Set the stroke or fill style. Like all path-drawing commands, you'll need to specify the fill or stroke style before drawing the arc.

2. Begin a path. Arcs, like lines, must be drawn as part of a path. Arcs can be combined with lines if you want.

3. Specify the center of the circle. An arc is simply a partial circle, so you begin defining an arc by determining the center of a circle. The first two parameters of the `arc()` method are the center of the circle.

4. Indicate the radius of the circle. The third parameter is the radius of the circle, which describes the arc.

5. Define beginning and ending points. An arc is a part of a circle. To indicate which part of the circle you want to draw, indicate the beginning and ending angles. These measurements are the fourth and fifth parameters of the `arc()` method. Note that angles are defined in radians.

6. Indicate the direction to draw. The last parameter determines the drawing direction. Use `true` for counter-clockwise, and `false` for clockwise.

The arc drawing functions are used in the following code:

```
function draw(){
  var drawing = document.getElementById("drawing");
  var con = drawing.getContext("2d");

  con.strokeStyle = "green";
  con.fillStyle = "rgba(255,0,0,0.5)";
```

```
con.lineWidth = "5";

//half-circle stroked
con.beginPath();
con.arc(220, 140, 50, 0, Math.PI, false);
con.closePath();
con.stroke();

//full circle filled
con.beginPath();
con.arc(220, 220, 50, 0, Math.PI*2, true);
con.closePath();
con.fill();
}
```

This code will generate the image shown in Figure 8-7.

Figure 8-7

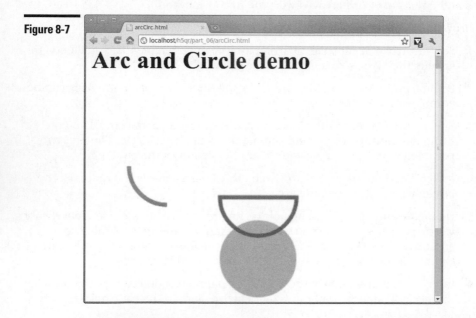

The angle measurements of the arc() command use *radians* as the unit of angle measurement. Radians are frequently used in mathematics rather than degrees. A radian is simply the angle described when you stretch the radius of a circle around the circumference of that same circle. Radians are normally expressed using the constant *pi* (π), so there are $2 \times \pi$ radians in a full circle. JavaScript has the built in constant Math.PI to simplify working with π. You can use the following chart to determine the main angles:

Direction	Angle
North	3 × Math.PI / 2
West	Math.PI
South	Math.PI / 2
East	0

If you're familiar with radian measurement, you might think the angles are upside down. (Typically, π / 2 is North, and 3 × π / 2 is South.) The angles are reversed because Y increases downwards in computer systems.

Making quadratic curves

The canvas element also supports two elegant curve-drawing mechanisms. A *quadratic curve* is a special curve with a starting and ending point. However, the line between the beginning and ending point is influenced by a *control point*. As an example, look at Figure 8-8. It shows a simple curve with a control point.

Figure 8-8

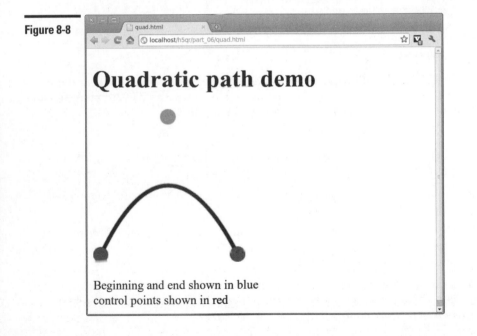

If you examine the code for the quadratic curve, you'll see it works much like drawing lines and arcs:

```
function draw(){
  drawing = document.getElementById("drawing");
  con = drawing.getContext("2d");

  con.strokeStyle = "black";
  con.lineWidth = "5";
  con.beginPath();
  con.moveTo(10,190);
  con.quadraticCurveTo(100, 10, 190, 190);
  con.stroke();
  con.closePath();

  //mark beginning and end with blue
  drawDot(10, 190, "blue");
  drawDot(190, 190, "blue");

  //mark control points with red
  drawDot(100, 10, "red");

} // end draw
```

The beginning and ending points of a quadratic curve are described explicitly, and the line begins and ends on these points. However, the control point doesn't usually lie on the curve. Instead, it *influences* the curve.

Here's how to build a quadratic curve:

1. Begin a path. Curves, like most drawing features, act in the context of a path.

2. Move to the starting position. Use the moveTo() command to move to where you want the curve to begin.

3. Use the quadraticCurveTo() method to draw the curve. This method takes four parameters: the X and Y position of the control point and the X and Y position of the end point.

4. Draw another curve if you want. Like most of the drawing commands, you can chain a series of quadraticCurveTo() calls together to build a more complex shape.

 Note that for this example I called a custom function called drawDot to draw the various points on the screen. See the complete code on my Web site (www.aharrisbooks.net/h5qr).

Producing a bezier curve

The *bezier curve* is another curve-drawing tool. It is similar to the quadratic curve, except it requires two control points. Figure 8-9 illustrates a bezier curve.

Figure 8-9

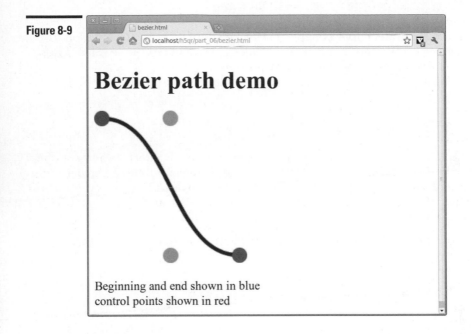

Building a bezier curve is almost exactly like building a quadratic curve. The `bezierCurveTo` function takes six parameters, the X and Y positions of control point one, control point two, and the ending point. Here's the code for the bezier path shown in Figure 8-9:

```
function draw(){
  drawing = document.getElementById("drawing");
  con = drawing.getContext("2d");

  con.strokeStyle = "black";
  con.lineWidth = "5";
  con.beginPath();
  con.moveTo(10,190);
  con.quadraticCurveTo(100, 10, 190, 190);
  con.stroke();
  con.closePath();

  //mark beginning and end with blue
  drawDot(10, 190, "blue");
```

```
        drawDot(190, 190, "blue");

        //mark control points with red
        drawDot(100, 10, "red");
    } // end draw
```

Like in the quadratic curve example, I used a custom `drawDot()` function to draw circles for the control point. *See* "Making arcs and circles," earlier in this part, for information on how to draw these dots.

Images

While HTML has long had support for images, the canvas interface adds new life to Web images. Images can be displayed inside a canvas, where they can be integrated with the vector-drawing techniques of the canvas API. You can also select a portion of an image to display, and apply the various transformations to your image to create interesting compositions and animations.

Figure 8-10 shows a basic version of this technique, with an image drawn twice on a canvas element.

Figure 8-10

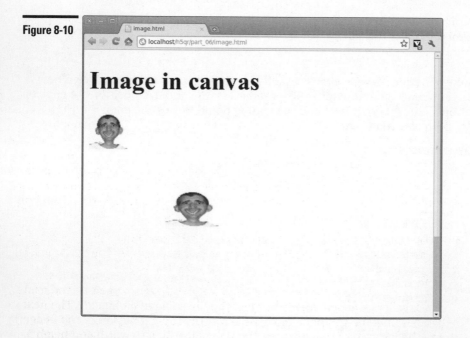

Drawing an image on the canvas

The easiest way to use an image in a canvas element is to use an image that is already available on the Web page. You can put an image on the page with the ordinary `<img>` tag and use the CSS `display: none` rule to make the image invisible. An alternate approach is to create an `Image` object in JavaScript and apply the `src` attribute to connect that image to a specific image file. For examples of both techniques, consider the following HTML code:

```
<img class = "hidden"
     id = "goofyPic"
     src = "andyGoofy.gif"
     alt = "Goofy pic of me" />

<canvas id = "drawing"
        height = "400"
        width = "400">
  <p>Canvas not supported</p>
</canvas>
```

The following JavaScript code displays the image in the canvas:

```
function draw(){
  var drawing = document.getElementById("drawing");
  var con = drawing.getContext("2d");
  var goofyPic = document.getElementById("goofyPic");
  con.drawImage(goofyPic, 0, 0, 50, 50);

  var image2 = new Image();
  image2.src = "andyGoofy.gif";
  con.drawImage(image2, 100, 100, 70, 50);
} // end draw
```

Here's how it's done:

1. **Create the image in the main page.** The easiest way to access an image is to use ordinary HTML to embed the image in the main page. If you want, you can hide the `<img>` tag with CSS code (`display: none`) so that only the version in the canvas is visible.

2. **Create a JavaScript variable for the image.** Use the ordinary `document.getElementByID()` mechanism to create a variable referring to the image.

3. **Draw the image on the canvas.** The `drawImage()` function takes five parameters. The first is the name of an image object. (It must be the name of a JavaScript image object, not just the file name of an image.) The next two parameters are the X and Y values of the top-left corner of the image, and the last two parameters are the size of the image (width and height).

4. Create a JavaScript `Image` object. If you don't want to embed an image in the page, you can use JavaScript to create an image dynamically. Use the `new Image()` constructor to build a new image.

5. Change the image's `src` property. If you create a JavaScript image, you must specify the `src` attribute to indicate the file associated with the image. It might take some time for the image to load.

The image won't display until it has loaded from the server. In most cases, this won't be a problem, but sometimes you'll find you need to delay your program until the image has finished loading. The `Image` object has an `onload` property that accepts a callback function. Use this technique to wait until your drawing finishes:

```
image.onload = finishDrawing;
function finishDrawing(){
 //rest of drawing code goes here
}
```

Drawing part of an image

Sometimes you'll want to draw a small part of the original image. Figure 8-11 illustrates a program focusing in on the center of the goofy face:

Figure 8-11

It's quite easy to draw part of an image. Use the same `drawImage()` command, but this time use a version with nine parameters:

```
con.drawImage(goofyPic, 60, 70, 90, 90, 0, 0, 150, 150);
```

Here's what all these parameters mean:

- **Image name:** The first parameter is the image object (not the filename, but the name of the JavaScript `Image` object).

- **Top-left corner of source:** The first job is to choose the part of the original picture that will be displayed. The next two parameters indicate the top-left corner of a selection on the original picture. (You might use an image editor like Gimp or IrfanView to determine the selection position and size.)

- **Height and width of source:** The next two parameters indicate the height and width of the source selection.

- **Position of destination:** The next two parameters are the position of the picture's top-left corner on the canvas.

- **Size of destination:** The last two parameters describe the size of the destination image on the canvas.

The subimage technique described here is quite useful because it allows you to combine several images into a single image (sometimes called a *sprite sheet*). This decreases the overhead for delivering the image. (One large image is faster to deliver than several small ones.) It's also frequently used in games and animations where one entity might have several images displayed in sequence to suggest walking or attacking.

Manipulating Images with Transformations

Transformations are math operations that can be applied to any drawing or image to change the appearance. There are three major transformations:

- **translation:** Moves a particular amount in X and Y.

- **rotation:** Rotates around a particular point.

- **scale:** Changes the size of the object in X and Y.

The canvas element allows all these operations on any type of drawing. However, the way the canvas element does this gets a little closer to math than you may have gotten before. Transformations in the canvas element can be hard to comprehend until you understand a little about how they really work.

In math, you don't really transform *objects*. Instead, you modify the *coordinate system* and draw your image in the newly transformed coordinate system. It's common in a vector-drawing application to have several hidden coordinate systems working at once. That's important because it's the way canvas transformations work. Essentially, when you want to perform transformations on an object, you'll do the following:

1. Announce the beginning of a temporary coordinate system. The main image already has its own coordinate system that won't change. Before you can transform anything, you need to build a new coordinate system to hold those changes. The (poorly named) `save()` command indicates the beginning of a new coordinate system definition.

2. Move the center with `translate()`. The origin (0, 0) starts in the upper-left corner of the canvas by default. Normally, you'll build your transformed objects on the (new) origin and move the origin to place the object. If you `translate(50, 50)` and then draw an image at (0, 0), the image will be drawn at the origin of the temporary coordinate system, which will be at (50, 50) in the main canvas.

3. Rotate the coordinate system with `rotate()`. The `rotate()` command rotates the new coordinate system around its origin. The rotation parameter is a degree in radians.

4. Scale the coordinate system in X and Y. You can also alter the new coordinate system by applying X and Y scale values. This allows you to create stretched and squashed images.

5. Create elements in the new coordinate system. Once you've applied all the transformations you want, you can use all the ordinary canvas drawing techniques. However, these drawings will be drawn in the virtual coordinate system you just made, not in the canvas' main coordinate system.

6. Close the temporary coordinate system. Generally you'll want to apply different transformations to different parts of your canvas. When you're finished with a particular transformation, use the `restore()` command to close out the new coordinate system. All subsequent drawing commands will use the default coordinate system of the canvas object.

Building a transformed image

A real example is easier to follow, so look at the code below:

```
function draw(){
  var drawing = document.getElementById("drawing");
  var con = drawing.getContext("2d");
  var goofyPic = document.getElementById("goofyPic");

  con.save();
```

```
con.translate(100, 100);
con.rotate(Math.PI / 4);
con.scale(3.0, 1.5);
con.drawImage(goofyPic, -25, -25, 50, 50);
con.restore();

//draw a rectangle using the ordinary coordinate system
con.strokeStyle = "red";
con.lineWidth = 5;
con.strokeRect(0, 0, 200, 200);

} // end draw
```

This program creates a new coordinate system containing a translation, rotation, and scale. It draws an image in the new coordinate system. It then reverts to the standard coordinate system and draws a rectangular frame.

This program features several transformations, as shown in Figure 8-12.

Figure 8-12

Here's how to build this type of image:

1. Get access to an image object. Load the image from the main site (as I have done in this example) or through JavaScript code. (*See* "Drawing an image on the canvas," earlier in this part.)

2. Start the transformation with the `save()` method. The `save()` method has (if you ask me) a very confusing name. This method *does not* save the canvas to a file. Instead, it saves the current coordinate system settings in memory and allows you to define a new coordinate system. I would have called this method `beginTransform()`.

3. Apply any translations you want. Remember, translations move the entire coordinate system. If you translate the coordinate system by (100, 100) as I did in this example, that means any subsequent drawings at (0, 0) will actually appear in the center of my 200 × 200 canvas.

4. Rotate the coordinate system if you want. You can apply a rotation to the coordinate system if you prefer. The system will rotate around its origin. Typically, to get the behavior you want, design your images so they are centered on the origin, and translate the origin to move the image. Rotation angles are defined in radians. If you're more comfortable with degrees, you can use this formula to convert: `radians = degrees × (Math.PI / 180)`.

5. Scale the coordinate system by X and Y. You can change the apparent width and height of your new coordinate system by indicating new scale values. Scaling is a multiplication operation. If the scale is one, the element stays the same size. If the scale is 2, the element is double the original size, and .5 is half the original size. You can even scale by a negative number to invert the image.

6. Draw your image. Draw on the canvas after you've applied all the transformations. You can do any canvas-drawing techniques you want: paths, rectangles, images, text, or whatever. The drawing will be modified by the indicated transformations.

7. End the transformation. The `restore()` method should be called `endTransform()`. (If you're listening, W3C, I'm available to help you come up with better names for things. Let me know when the meetings are scheduled.) Regardless, this method indicates that you're done thinking about all the transformations that have been declared in this transform, and you're ready to return to the default coordinate system. The term *restore* really means "return to the coordinate state that was saved with the `save` command that was called to begin this transformation."

8. Subsequent drawings will use the default coordinates. In my example, I draw an ordinary rectangle around the image. This rectangle should use the regular coordinates of the canvas — I don't want it rotated or scaled like the image. Since these drawing commands exist outside the context of the `save()`/`restore()` pair, they use the regular coordinate system.

Some key points about transformations

Transformations are an incredibly powerful tool set, and they're among the most anticipated features of HTML5. However, they do hide a certain amount of math. You can use them without understanding linear algebra (the underlying mathematical theory), but there's still a few key ideas to keep in mind:

- ✔ **Each transformation is stored as a matrix.** There's an underlying structure called a *matrix* (that's even cooler than the movie) which stores all the translations, rotations, and scales in a single mathematical structure. You can work with the transformation matrix directly if you prefer, with the context objects' `transform()` method.

- ✔ **The order of transformations makes a difference.** Try this experiment. Stand in the center of the room. Now go forward five steps and turn left 90 degrees. Look at where you are. Now go back to the same starting point. This time, turn left 90 degrees and then go forward five steps. Are you in the same place? You might need to experiment a bit to get things working the way you expect.

- ✔ **Transform the system and then draw on the origin.** Most of the drawing commands in canvas allow you to draw things anywhere on the canvas. If you're not using transformations, you can use this mechanism to place things wherever you want. However, if you're using a transformation, it's much easier to transform the entire coordinate system and then draw your elements at the origin (0, 0). Otherwise you'll get some very strange results (especially with combined rotations and translations).

Using Animation

Of course, the big question about the HTML5 canvas tag is whether it can replace Flash as a mechanism for implementing games and animations in the browser. The jury is still out on this, but it is reasonably easy to add animation to a canvas image. The key is to use the animation features already built into the browser.

Basic structure of the animation loop

An animation generally requires a special organization called an *animation loop*. The basic structure of the animation loop works the same in any language:

1. Initialization. Create the assets, including the background and any of the objects you will be using. Objects that will be manipulated in real time are normally called *sprites*. Generally, this is done when the program first runs, to save time during the main execution. You may also set constants for image size, display size, frame rate, and other values that will not change during the execution of the game.

2. Determine a frame rate. Animations and games work by calling a function repeatedly at a prescribed rate. In general, you'll have some sort of function that is called repeatedly. In JavaScript, you typically use the `set Interval()` function to specify a function that will be called repeatedly. The *frame rate* indicates how often the specified function will be called. Games and animations typically run at frame rates between 10 and 30 frames per second. A faster frame rate is smoother, but may not be maintainable with some hardware.

3. Evaluate the current state. Each sprite is really a data element. During every frame, determine if anything important has happened: Did the user press a key? Is an element supposed to move? Did a sprite leave the screen? Did two sprites conk into each other?

4. Modify sprite data. Each sprite generally has position or rotation data that can be modified during each frame. Usually this is done through transformations (translation, rotation, and scale) although sometimes you may switch between images instead.

5. Clear the background. An animation is really a series of images drawn rapidly in the same place. Usually, you'll need to clear the background at the beginning of each frame to clear out the last frame's image.

6. Redraw all sprites. Each sprite is redrawn using its new data. The sprites appear to move because they're drawn in a new location or orientation.

Typically, I would display a screen shot here, but a still image of an animation won't be fun to look at in this book. Please look at `autoRotate.html` on my Web site (`www.aharrisbooks.net/h5qr`) to see the program running in real time. While you're at it, check out all the other great stuff I've got on that site for you.

Creating the constants

As an example, build a program that rotates an image inside a canvas. The complete code is in several parts. I'll use a basic image as a sprite. The first job is to set up the various variables and constants that describe the problem. The following code is created outside any functions because it describes values that will be shared among functions:

```
var drawing;
var con;
var goofyPic;
var angle = 0;
CANV_HEIGHT = 200;
CANV_WIDTH = 200;
SPR_HEIGHT = 50;
SPR_WIDTH = 40;
```

The `drawing` variable will refer to the `canvas` element. The `con` variable will be the drawing context, `goofyPic` is the image to be rotated, and `angle` will be used to determine how much the image is currently rotated. The other values are constants used to describe the height and width of the canvas as well as the sprite.

Deploying the animation

As usual, the `body onload` mechanism will be used to start up some code as soon as the page has finished loading. However, the page now has two functions. The `init()` function handles initialization, and the `draw()` function will be called repeatedly to handle the actual animation. Here's the code in the `init()` function:

```
function init(){
    drawing = document.getElementById("drawing");
    con = drawing.getContext("2d");
    goofyPic = document.getElementById("goofyPic");
    setInterval(draw, 100);
} // end init
```

The job of the `init()` function is to initialize things. In this particular example, I load up the various elements (the canvas, the context, and the image) into JavaScript variables, and I set up the animation. The `setInterval()` function is used to set up the main animation loop. It takes two parameters:

- **A repeatable function:** The first parameter is the name of a function which will be called repeatedly. In this case, I will be calling the `draw` function many times.

- **A delay value:** The second parameter indicates how often the function should be called in milliseconds (1/1000 of a second). A delay of 100 will create a frame rate of 10 frames per second. A delay of 50 will cause a frame rate of 20 frames per second, and so on.

Giving animation to the current frame

The `draw()` function will be called many times in succession. In general, its task is to clear the frame, calculate new sprite states, and redraw the sprite. Here's the code:

```
function draw(){

    //clear background
    con.fillStyle = "white";
    con.fillRect(0, 0, CANV_HEIGHT, CANV_WIDTH);

    //draw border
    con.strokeStyle = "red";
    con.lineWidth = "5";
```

```
    con.strokeRect(0, 0, CANV_WIDTH, CANV_HEIGHT);

    //change the rotation angle
    angle += .25;
    if (angle > Math.PI * 2){
      angle = 0;
    }

    //start a new transformation system
    con.save();
    con.translate(100, 100);
    con.rotate(angle);

    //draw the image
    con.drawImage(goofyPic,
        SPR_WIDTH/-2, SPR_HEIGHT/-2,
        SPR_WIDTH, SPR_HEIGHT);
      con.restore();
  } // end draw
```

While the code may seem a little involved, it doesn't really do anything new:

1. Clear the background. Remember that animation is repeated drawing. If you don't clear the background at the beginning of every frame, you'll see the previous frame drawings. Use the context's `clearRect()` function to draw a fresh background, or one of the other drawing tools to use a more complex background image. You must clear the background first, so subsequent drawings will happen on a fresh palette.

2. Draw any nonsprite content. In this example, I want a red border around the frame. Just use ordinary canvas elements for this. I used `stroke Style`, `lineWidth`, and `strokeRect()` to build a red rectangular frame around my canvas. Note that I used the CANV_HEIGHT and CANV_WIDTH constants to refer to the current canvas size.

3. Modify the sprite state. In this example, I want to modify the rotation angle of the image. I already created a variable called `angle` outside the function. (It's important that `angle` was created outside the function context so it can retain its value between calls to the function.) I add a small amount to `angle` every frame. Whenever you change a variable (especially in a virtually endless loop like an animation), you should check for boundary conditions. In this example, I'm changing angles. The largest permissible angle value (in radians) is $2 \times \pi$. If the angle gets larger than $2 \times \pi$, it is reset to zero.

4. Build a transformation. Many animations are really modifications of a transformation. That's the case here. I'm actually not changing the image at all, but the transformation that contains the image. Set up a new transformation with the `save()` method, and use the `rotate()` and `translate()` functions to transform a temporary coordinate system. (See "Manipulating Images with Transformations," earlier in this part, for information on how transformations relate to temporary coordinate systems.

5. Draw the image at the center of the new transformation. Remember, the `drawImage()` command draws the image based on the top-left corner of an image. If you draw the image at (0, 0) of the new transformation, the image will appear to rotate around its top-left corner. Usually, you'll want an image to rotate around its center point. Simply draw the image so its center is at the origin. Set X to zero minus half the image's width, and Y to zero minus half the image's height.

6. Close the transformation. Use the `restore()` method to finish defining the temporary coordinate system.

Moving an element

Often you'll prefer to move an element. This process is actually very similar to the rotation mechanism. Here's some code that moves an image and wraps it to the other side when it leaves the canvas:

```
var drawing;
var con;
var goofyPic;
CANV_HEIGHT = 200;
CANV_WIDTH = 200;
SPR_HEIGHT = 50;
SPR_WIDTH = 40;

var x = 0;
var y = 100;
var dx = 10;
var dy = 7;

function init(){
  drawing = document.getElementById("drawing");
  con = drawing.getContext("2d");
  goofyPic = document.getElementById("goofyPic");
  setInterval(draw, 100);
}

function draw(){
```

```
    //clear background
    con.clearRect(0, 0, 200, 200);

    //move the element
    x += dx;
    y += dy;

    //check for boundaries
    wrap();

    //draw the image
    con.drawImage(goofyPic, x, y, SPR_WIDTH, SPR_HEIGHT);

    //draw a rectangle
    con.strokeStyle = "red";
    con.lineWidth = 5;
    con.strokeRect(0, 0, CANV_WIDTH, CANV_HEIGHT);

} // end draw

function wrap(){
    if (x > CANV_WIDTH){
        x = 0;
    }
    if (x < 0){
        x = CANV_WIDTH;
    }
    if (y > CANV_HEIGHT){
        y = 0;
    } // end if
    if (y < 0){
        y = CANV_HEIGHT;
    }
} // end wrap
```

The `wrap` code is very similar to the rotation program. It has a few different features:

  ✔ **Keep track of the sprite position.** The sprite's position will change now, so the important variables are x and y, used to track where the sprite is.

  ✔ **You also need variables for the sprite's motion.** The dx variable stands for *difference in x,* and it is used to show how much the x value changes each frame. Likewise, dy is used to show how much the y value changes in each frame. x, y, dx, and dy are all created outside the function context.

✔ **Move the element values.** In every frame (in the draw() function) add dx to x and add dy to y.

✔ **Check for boundaries.** I created a new function called wrap() to check for boundary conditions. The code is pretty straightforward. If the sprite's x value exceeds the width of the canvas (meaning it has moved to the right border of the canvas), reset the x value to 0 (moving it to the left). Use a similar calculation to check the other borders and reset the image to the opposite side.

Once again, a static still image will not show justice to this animation. Please look at wrap.html on my Web site (www.aharrisbooks.net/h5qr) to see an example. The bounce.html page shows the bounce example in the next section.

Now we're bouncing off the walls

If you prefer to have your sprite bounce off the walls, just replace the wrap() function with a bounce() function that works like this:

```
function bounce(){
  if (x > CANV_WIDTH - SPR_WIDTH){
    dx *= -1;
  }
  if (x < 0){
    dx *= -1;
  }
  if (y > CANV_HEIGHT - SPR_HEIGHT){
    dy *= -1;
  }
  if (y < 0){
    dy *= -1;
  }
} // end bounce
```

Working with Pixel Manipulation

The canvas tag has one more incredible trick up its sleeve. You can extract the data of a canvas tag into the underlying pixel data. If you know how to manipulate this data, you can have very extensive control of your image in real time. You can use this data for color balancing, as well as experimenting with your own blurs, sharpens, and chroma-key effects.

In order to understand what this is doing, you need to have some knowledge of how pictures are stored in memory. No matter what format an image is stored in on the file system, it is displayed as a list of pixels. Each pixel is represented (in the standard 32-bit system, anyway) by four integers: RGBA. The R value represents how much red is in the current dot. G stands for green, and B stands for blue. The A stands for *alpha,* which is a measure of the transparency of the image. Each of these values can vary from 0 to 255. When you convert an image to the image data format, you get a huge array of integers. Each group of four images represents a single pixel of color data.

Here's an example that changes the color balance of an image:

```
function draw(){
 var drawing = document.getElementById("drawing");
 var con = drawing.getContext("2d");
 var original = document.getElementById("original");

 CANV_WIDTH = 200;
 CANV_HEIGHT = 200;

 //draw the original on the canvas
 con.drawImage(original, 0, 0);

 //get the image data
 imgData = con.getImageData(0, 0, 200, 200);

 //loop through image data
 for (row = 0; row < CANV_HEIGHT; row++){
   for (col = 0; col < CANV_WIDTH; col++){
     //find current pixel
     index = (col + (row * imgData.width)) * 4;

     //separate into color values
     r = imgData.data[index];
     g = imgData.data[index + 1];
     b = imgData.data[index + 2];
     a = imgData.data[index + 3];

     //manipulate color values
     r -= 20;
     g += 50;
     b -= 30;
     a = a;

     //manage boundary conditions
     if (r > 255){
       r = 255;
     }
     if (r < 0){
```

```
      r = 0;
   }
   if (g > 255){
      g = 255;
   }
   if (g < 0){
      g = 0;
   }
   if (b > 255){
      r = 255;
   }
   if (b < 0){
      b = 0;
   }
   if (a > 255){
      a = 255;
   }
   if (a < 0){
      a = 0;
   }

   //return new values to data
   imgData.data[index] = r;
   imgData.data[index+1] = g;
   imgData.data[index+2] = b;
   imgData.data[index+3] = a;
 } // end col for loop
} // end row for loop

//draw new image onto canvas
con.putImageData(imgData, 0, 0);

} // end function
```

While the code listing seems quite long, it really isn't too difficult to follow:

1. **Draw an original image.** The technique you'll use extracts data from a canvas element, so to modify an image you first need to draw it onto a canvas. I drew my goofy face image on the canvas first with the ordinary `drawImage()` method.

2. **Extract the image data.** The `getImageData()` method gets the picture displayed by the current canvas and places it in a huge array of integers.

3. **Make a loop to handle the rows.** Image data is broken into rows and columns. Each row goes from 0 to the height of the canvas, so make a `for` loop to iterate through the rows.

4. Make another loop to handle the columns. Inside each row is enough data to go from 0 to the width of the canvas, so make a second for loop inside the first. It's very common to use a pair of nested for loops to step through two-dimensional data like image information.

5. Find the index in `imageData` for the current row and column. The `imageData` array contains four integers for each pixel, so we have to do a little math to figure out where the first integer for each pixel is. The easiest formula is to multiply the row number by the width of the canvas, add that to the column number, and multiply the entire result by four.

6. Pull the corresponding color values from the index. The index also represents the red value of the current pixel. The next `int` holds the green value, followed by the blue value, and finally the alpha value.

7. Manipulate the color values as you want. If you're going to do a color-balancing app (as I'm doing), you can simply add or subtract values to change the overall color balance. In my example, I add a bit to green and subtract a bit from red and blue. I chose to leave the alpha alone. Of course, this is where you can do much more elaborate work if you want to play around with pixel-level image manipulation.

8. Check for boundaries. A pixel value cannot be lower than 0 or higher than 255, so check for both of these boundaries and adjust all pixel values to be within legal limits

9. Return manipulated values back to the `imgData` array. You can copy values back to the array, and you should do so to make the changes visible.

10. Draw the image data back to the canvas. The `putImageData()` function draws the current image data back to the canvas as an ordinary image. The new version of the image will reflect the changes. In my case, I have a decidedly ill-looking image.

Color-balancing is too subtle an effect to display accurately in a black-and-white screen shot, so please visit my Web site (`www.aharrisbooks.net/h5qr`) to see this program in its full glory.

Index